RED
EGGS
AND
GOOD
LUCK

RED EGGS AND GOOD LUCK

ANGELA LAM

SHE WRITES PRESS

Published 2015
Printed in the United States of America
ISBN: 978-1-63152-005-1
Library of Congress Control Number: 2015936270

For information, address:
She Writes Press
1563 Solano Ave #546
Berkeley, CA 94707

She Writes Press is a division of SparkPoint Studio, LLC.

Names and identifying characteristics have been changed to protect the privacy of certain individuals.

To Dad, Mom, Cynthia, Elizabeth, and Sylvia

And in loving memory of
John C. Lam and Lillian A. Lam

1: THE MAKEOVER

I am eleven, not quite a little girl, not quite a young woman. There are things I know that I should not know, things of which I am not to speak, such as: I am not supposed to know my father works as a checkout clerk, not the grocery store manager. I am not supposed to know the dolls I play with are stolen. I am not supposed to know my parents have gambled away the second mortgage on the house instead of investing it in a new toilet, a shower with working doors, dual-pane windows, and a new roof. I am supposed to be a China doll, silent and submissive, an example to my sisters: Cynthia, eight, and Elizabeth, six.

The day before my uncle's birthday party, my father, Chee, packs our family into the brown-and-beige Club Wagon van and shuttles us to the Valley Fair Shopping Mall in Santa Clara, where my sisters and I will have our hair cut and permed. "To look American, like Lammie Pie," he says, referring to our mother, with her golden-brown hair and crystal-blue eyes. Ever since he was an immigrant boy growing up in San Francisco's Chinatown, my father has been in love with American movies and movie stars. He swears he married my mother because she looked like Doris Day. My mother, born at the end of World War II, nine years after my father, is no longer blonde and slender. After three children, she grew round and stopped highlighting her hair and taking dance lessons and going out after work for a drink with the girls. But I still think of her as beautiful. In her wedding photos, with her sleek white gown and diamond tiara, she looks like Miss America.

My father, whose American name is Dave Lam, is a wizened brown man, who smoothes glossy pomade through his Elvis hair. When people ask, "What nationality are you?" he says, "Hawaiian, like Don Ho, the singer." And, in his awkward voice, he'll sing "Tiny Bubbles." As a child, he wanted to dance like Fred Astaire and tell jokes like Jack Benny. When that failed, he embarked on a quest to find an American wife. With an American wife, he reasoned, he could be a star. After moving to San Jose, he met my mother in the checkout line at the grocery store where he worked. (The Chinese checker, he called himself.) He had trouble pronouncing her name, Margaret, so after they married, he called her Lammie Pie. "Lammie," he explained, "because she's my little Lam. And Pie because it's my favorite dessert." Though my mother calls him Dave, my sisters and I think of him as Chee.

On the way to the beauty parlor, Chee rolls through a four-way stop, punches the gas, and nearly rams the center divide as he careens onto the freeway.

"Slow down," Lammie Pie says.

"Aiyaah, we can't be late."

Our appointment is for two thirty. At two fifteen the van lurches over a curb and into an empty parking space at the far end of the Valley Fair Shopping Mall. "Don't want anyone scratching the paint job," Chee says. He hops out of the van and arches his back. The vertebrae snap into place. He sniffs the smell of hamburgers and french fries from McDonald's, and rubs his stomach. "Smells good. Too bad we already had lunch."

Cynthia and Elizabeth hold hands and follow Chee's long strides through the rows of cars. I stay behind with Lammie Pie, waiting for her to roll up the windows and lock the doors.

Chee calls to me, "Angela, what are you waiting for? We'll be late."

Lammie Pie shoos me along. "Go after your father. You don't want him to be angry, do you?"

I gaze at my mother's frowning face. "I want to be with you," I say, groping for her hand.

Lammie Pie glowers, cutting through any tenderness I may have been feeling. "I'll be right behind you. Now go."

I lope ahead of my sisters, who look like twins with their long black hair and matching dresses, which Lammie Pie sewed while watching *The Price Is Right* on TV. I am wearing a green store-bought dress, a gift from my mother's sister Mildred for getting straight A's three quarters in a row. "Green brings out the color of your eyes," Aunt Mildred said, tucking the collar under my chin. "You have your grandfather's eyes. Hazel. They change with the light. Elizabeth and Cynthia, they have their father's dark eyes. They absorb the light. Nothing comes out."

I like Aunt Mildred. She hates my father.

At the door, we wait for Lammie Pie to catch up. She huffs and puffs. The knit top she sewed from a Butterick's pattern clings to her bosom, and the pastel-blue polyester pants Chee shoplifted from Montgomery Ward last week are an inch too short for her legs. In the wind her perm turns into matted brown fuzz and sticks up like gnarled weeds.

Cynthia and Elizabeth tilt their heads together and titter behind cupped hands. Chee slaps their shoulders. "What's so funny? Have you no respect for your mother?"

We step into Macy's, and a blast of perfume assaults us. I sneeze. Chee stops at the cosmetic counter and asks about a makeover. The blonde sales clerk examines Lammie Pie.

"No, not that one. *This* one." He points to me.

"She doesn't need anything," the clerk says. "She's just a child."

"She's almost a teenager. She's going to a party. She needs makeup."

He pulls me toward the counter. I jerk my arm away and gaze up at him with pleading eyes. "Dad, I don't want to."

"Go. Listen to the nice lady. She's going to make you look beautiful. Like a movie star." Ever since my father discovered that I cannot play the piano or dance, his only hope has been for me to become beautiful.

The clerk gazes sympathetically at me and leads me to a stool beside the glass counters. Gleaming black-and-gold tubes of lipstick and mascara with expensive price tags wink up at me. Chee tells Lammie Pie to take the girls to the beauty salon. We will meet them there when we are done. I watch Lammie Pie, the white Buddha, lead my black-haired sisters, each holding one of her hands, as if for luck. I want to follow them up the escalator to the top floor and sit on a vinyl chair, flipping through glossy magazines.

"Look up," the clerk says, lifting my chin. "Close your eyes half-way." Her hands are softly perfumed. She brushes my lids with a topaz glitter.

"No," Chee says. "Something darker."

"Darker? She doesn't need darker."

"Yes. Something dark."

The clerk sighs, takes out a compact with quartz eye shadow, and brushes it over the topaz.

Chee smiles. "Much better."

The clerk shakes a tube of mascara and tells me to close my eyes again. She brushes black over the lashes until my eye lids feel heavy.

"Good," Chee says.

The clerk applies a peach blush across my cheekbones.

Again Chee says, "No, darker."

The clerk frowns and sorts through an array of colors.

"Yes, red. That's it," Chee says, smiling.

"She won't look good in it."

"She'll look beautiful."

The clerk brushes my cheeks with Just Right Red. Then she selects a pink gloss for my lips.

"No, same color as the cheeks."

"You want her to look like a woman?" the clerk asks. "She's just a baby."

"Darker. I buy everything she has on and more."

The clerk crosses her arms, considering the offer, then ruffles through her samples for a lusty red. She puckers her lips to show me how to pucker mine. The soft red tube smears over them like a moist finger.

"How's that?" the clerk asks.

"Beautiful. She looks like a movie star."

The clerk hands me a mirror. I gaze into a stranger's face: the dark eyes, the swollen cheeks, the flaming mouth. Tears well up, but I do not let them show. In a way, I am glad I look different. No one will recognize me. I can pretend I am anyone, do anything. I can be like my father, who lives without consequences.

Chee pays $150 for the makeup I am wearing. He flirts with the clerk, caressing her hand as he counts out the fifty-dollar bills into her palm: "Fifty for you, sweetheart, fifty for your dear mother, and fifty for making my daughter look like a Charlie's Angel." With his other hand, Chee slips samples from the counter into his pocket like spare change. When the clerk is not looking, he swipes a few more items from the counter, small bottles of perfume and foundation, cleansers and toners, and drops them into the shopping bag. He smiles phonily at the clerk, who hands him the receipt and pats my hand. "Good luck," she says.

I want to hit her. Luck is something the Chinese live and die by. I do not want to be blessed with good luck in front of my father. He may seize it for himself and leave me with nothing.

"See, that wasn't so bad." Chee swings the bag with one hand and wraps his other arm around me as if I were his girlfriend. He whistles a Frank Sinatra tune off key. I gaze the other way, pretending I do not know him. I'm ashamed of how I look, of whom I'm with. As we ride the escalator up, passersby stare disapprovingly. Chee squeezes my shoulder and tugs me closer, as if I might break free.

At the beauty salon my sisters sit side by side under the hair dryers. Lammie Pie is reading a recipe for double-chocolate soufflé in *McCall's*. She glances up from the magazine and takes in my transformation. "She looks just like you," Chee teases, and he touches her cheek.

Her frown deepens into a curious blend of disgust and envy, an expression I have never seen before. Chee does not notice. He hands her a trial-size bottle of perfume. She ignores it. Her blue-hot stare threatens to melt the wax-doll face I wear.

"I didn't want to do it," I say.

Chee smiles. "Don't you think she looks beautiful, Lammie Pie? Doesn't she look like a Charlie's Angel?"

Lammie Pie doesn't answer. Her stare causes me more shame than any stranger's could.

"I didn't want to do it," I repeat.

A beautician calls my name and leads me to the swivel chairs and mirrors.

Chee hustles over as the beautician wraps a tissue around my neck and drapes a burgundy cloth over my front.

"What do you want done today?" she asks.

"Cut and permed," Chee says. "Make her look like Shirley Temple."

This is what he always says. No matter what salon he takes us to, the perms always fall into stinky wet spirals around our pudgy faces and then dry into lightning bolts that stick up all over our heads if we don't sleep with rollers in our wet hair every night.

The beautician glances at Chee. "I asked her, sir, not you."

"I'm her father. I'm paying. She needs to look pretty for her uncle's birthday party tomorrow. And she looks good with a cut and perm. Just like her sisters." He points to Cynthia and Elizabeth, who are having the curlers taken from their hair.

The beautician fluffs her fingers through the hair at the nape of my neck. "I think a little body might be good," she says. "Her hair is rather thick."

"Not body. Curls."

The beautician nods. "Go have a seat, and I'll come get you when she's done, okay?"

When Chee leaves, I gaze at my face in the mirror. The makeup doesn't change my almond-shaped eyes or my yellowish skin. I sigh. I will always be half white, half Chinese. I will never be an American-style beauty.

The beautician pinches my cheeks and says, "You don't need so much makeup, honey. You're pretty just the way you are."

My chest tightens. *I didn't want the makeup.* Tears stream down my cheeks.

The beautician does not ask why I am crying. She grabs a damp washcloth from the sink and dabs at the black rivers running from my eyes. She catches my eye in the mirror and whispers, "I know you didn't want it. Just like you don't want this cut and perm."

I nod and sniff. Finally, someone who understands.

"But your dad's right. You're still a minor. When you grow up, though, you can wear your hair however you choose, do whatever you want. Can you remember that for me?"

I nod, not sure how long I will remember. But for the moment I feel better. And with the makeup muted by tears and warm water, my face doesn't look so strange anymore.

2: UNCLE JOHN'S BIRTHDAY PARTY

I don't want to go to Uncle John's sixtieth-birthday party. I don't want to sit around a Lazy Susan and eat mouthful after mouthful of strange food and smile at second cousins twice removed who speak broken English and fluent Cantonese. But it's no good pretending to be ill. Last year Elizabeth had the flu, and she had to come anyway. "I don't trust sitters," Chee said. "They feed you dog food and give you bath in dirty water." Why couldn't we all stay home, we asked. "If we don't go," he said, "we don't get money."

Lammie Pie says Chee doesn't know the Depression ended decades ago. "We aren't poor," she tells him. "We're middle class." But Chee doesn't listen. He always needs more money, and he doesn't care where the money comes from—sending our mother back to work as a bank teller, clipping coupons from the *San Jose Mercury News*, cashing in our Christmas savings bonds (which were meant for college), gambling at blackjack tables in Lake Tahoe, or begging handouts from his wealthy brothers. And as soon as the money is spent—on a brand-new car, or new shoes for our mother, or private tennis lessons for us girls—Chee needs more. Now.

My sisters and I curl our freshly permed hair and slip into the cotton dresses Lammie Pie has spent every night of the last three weeks sewing. In the tiny pink hallway bathroom, Cynthia, Elizabeth, and I jostle each other in front of the mirror. It reminds me of being backstage at a 4-H modeling show, only tonight the show is just for family, which makes it even more stressful, and more important to impress.

At a quarter to three, Chee screams, "Aiyaah! We don't want to be late! Get into the van!"

My sisters and I go to the bathroom one last time before filing into the Club Wagon. Cynthia and I sit in the captain's seats. Elizabeth sits on the big bench seat in the back, which converts into a bed so we can sleep on the ride home. Lammie Pie brings her cross-stitch and back issues of *McCall's*, *Family Circle*, and *Woman's Day*, although she will spend the entire trip navigating for Chee using the Bay Area map she picked up at AAA.

My mother, my sisters, and I love to listen to music, but Chee prefers AM talk radio. He flips from station to station until he finds a topic that interests him. At stoplights, he takes notes on a pad of paper glued to the dashboard beside a medallion of the Sacred Heart of Jesus and a box of tissue. He writes down quotes, titles of books, and noteworthy facts.

"Can't we listen to music?" Lammie Pie asks, as we turn onto the freeway.

"Why? It teaches you nothing. This guy talking right now has a PhD in economics from Harvard. He knows what's happening in the economy. Shh! Listen and learn."

Lammie Pie sighs and takes out her cross-stitch. While Chee believes in learning about the stock market and current events, Lammie Pie believes in the romance and heartbreak of love. At home, when Chee is at work, she listens to the Eagles' "Lyin' Eyes" and Kenny Rogers's "Ruby, Don't Take Your Love to Town." I listen and learn about the dark side of love, determined to find a happily-ever-after when I grow up.

At a quarter to five, Chee snaps off the radio and barks, "Check your hair. Check your makeup. Practice your smiles. Remember what I taught you to say." He parks the van, and we shuffle into the Chinese restaurant wearing our puffy-sleeved pastel dresses with the ribbon sashes. Our curled hair looks fluffy and soft, but it's stiff and dry and reeks of chemicals and hair spray. Cynthia and Elizabeth wear lip gloss, and I wear quartz eye shadow and Just

Right Red blush and lipstick. Lammie Pie applied the makeup while Chee stood over her, watching each stroke, commanding her to put on more and more. I look like a Chinese opera singer with a cowgirl hairdo.

Lammie Pie is the only white person at the restaurant. She sashays in wearing a blue satin gown and a diamond teardrop necklace that Chee bought with money he won in Tahoe two years ago. Chee has on one of Uncle John's hand-me-down brown wool suits. It's two sizes too small, but my mother has taken down the hems and cuffs, and patched the threadbare elbows. My father strides into the banquet hall like a king with his entourage. We follow him through a maze of white-linen-covered tables topped with buckets of ice and 7UP and Seagram's 7.

Uncle John, the guest of honor, is a tired-looking man with small brown eyes swimming in yellowed whites, big overlapping lips, and a sunken jaw. His concave body is mummified in a dark-gray suit. I know him mostly from infrequent visits to his house and grocery store, annual family get-togethers, and the stories Chee has told us. Chee's favorite story about Uncle John is how he could have married a poor seamstress, but instead he chose to marry a wealthy scholar, who is now mysteriously ill. "See how unhappy he is," Chee said. "Wife can't work, can't sew, can't do nothing. Just stay at home sick. Money's not everything. You marry for love." And he kissed Lammie Pie and patted her on the butt to demonstrate that he married for the right reason.

At the head table, Uncle John and my father talk in Cantonese: short, choppy sentences punctuated with hand gestures. My sisters and I do not speak Cantonese. Cynthia and Elizabeth stare at me with "What should we do?" expressions. When Chee motions to us, I grab their hands and lead them toward Uncle John. I hug him first, then Cynthia does, and finally Elizabeth. Uncle John smiles when he squeezes Elizabeth, who is soft and chubby from eating too many of the bear claws Chee brings home from the store. Elizabeth breaks away from Uncle John and stomps over to Cynthia, who refuses to hold her hand. Cynthia is strangely aloof and, like Lammie Pie, doesn't like to be cuddled or touched. Failing to get Cynthia's sympathy, Elizabeth sidles up to me. I wrap my arms around her and give her a hug.

Chee herds us to a table near the front, where the waiters are preparing the red eggs for my uncle. "Red eggs are a symbol of rebirth," Chee tells us. "When you turn sixty, you are born again. Like a baby. Only this time you are born into wisdom." He pockets one of the red eggs when the waiters are not looking. Lammie Pie glowers at him, and he shrugs. "Don't worry," he says. "Hard-boiled."

We sit at a round table near the center of the room, and the waiters bring platter after platter of food: wontons, sweet-and-sour pork, lemon chicken, cashew chicken, tomato-beef chow mein, roast duck, steamed rice, shrimp chips, shark soup, and rice pudding. Chee scoops up noodles with his chopsticks and slams them down on our plates. "Good for you," he says. "Make you strong."

The more I eat, the tighter the seams of my dress stretch over my stomach. My bladder sloshes from one too many glasses of 7UP, and I lean back to relieve the pressure.

The speeches start, first in Cantonese, then in English.

I tap my mother's arm. "Can I go to the restroom?" I ask.

My mother shakes her head and returns her gaze to the podium. I crane my neck, but I can't see over the bobbing, black-haired heads. Elizabeth tries to stand on her seat to look, but Chee yanks her down and curses at her in English.

I wave to a waiter, who balances empty platters on his long arms. He bends down and asks, "What do you need?"

"Where's the restroom?" I whisper.

He points to the door beside the kitchen on the other side of the room. I calculate the distance. I will have to pass five tables of people who might recognize me from the school photos Chee has sent them over the years. I don't want them to stare at me and think, *Why she not sit down? Her American mother let her do as she please. What a shame!* I imagine my father making excuses for me, to hide his embarrassment, and the bitter, stinging words on the ride home: "Couldn't you have waited just five minutes? I told you to go to the bathroom before we left. Were you not listening?"

I wonder what I should do. I don't want to offend my father, which is easy to do. He is a bundle of contradictions. "It's not my fault," he once told us. "I've lived two lives. In the morning, I went to Chinese school. The teachers called me 'Lam Chee Ning.' In the afternoon, I went to American school. The nuns called me 'Dave Lam.' I tried to follow the Ten Commandments, but I fought a lot. Too many people don't like us Chinese." Whenever a situation arises, I don't know which side of my father will respond: Chee or Dave, the Chinese fighter or the American lover. I decide to stay seated until the speeches are over. I clutch my stomach and feel my swollen bladder. Maybe if I don't move or breathe, I'll be all right.

Peering between people's shoulders, I glimpse a banner someone has presented to Uncle John. Chee turns around and explains, "It's written in Chinese, in red and gold, for happiness and good luck."

Chopsticks click against the sides of teacups. Everyone stands and lifts his or her glass for a toast. "Happy birthday, John! Here's to another sixty years!"

I tug on the waistband of my dress, but it is my skin that is too tight, not the sash. I rock my feet back and forth, trying to take my mind off the uncomfortable fullness of my stomach and bladder.

The party ends. Guests shuffle toward the coat room for their belongings. I search for a path to the restroom, but my father pinches my elbow. "Go hug Uncle John," he says. "Wish him good luck. If he asks what you need, tell him money for braces and dance lessons for your sister."

"I have to go to the restroom," I say.

"Later." Chee shoves me toward the podium. "Go hug Uncle John first."

My mother leans down and says, "Your father already tried talking to him, but he wouldn't listen."

From my mother's sorrowful expression, I know the earlier conversation between Uncle John and my father involved money. I imagine what my father must have said: "I work so hard, I almost die of an ulcer." It's true, I know, but Uncle John must have glared at him, thinking Chee was playing on his sympathies and the memory of their father, who did die of an ulcer.

Now it is up to me and my sisters to convince Uncle John that we are worthy of any money he might give us. We make our way over to where Uncle John sits with an elbow on the table and one finger tapping his chin. His forehead is furrowed. He smiles when he sees us, but the creases do not go away. His gaze lingers over our pale skin, our half-slanted eyes, our American bodies clothed in pastels, not the dark silks his crippled wife wears. I wonder if he sees us as family or just the daughters of an American sister-in-law.

He stands up, and Elizabeth hugs him first. When it is my turn, I press myself against the scratchy wool of his coat and hold my breath against the stench of spoiled fish.

Uncle John tells Cynthia and Elizabeth to go to Lammie Pie and wait for me. "I want to talk to Angela," he says. His claw-like hands tremble as he pulls back a chair. "Sit," he says.

I obey, smoothing my dress over my full bladder. Being taller than he is, I can see the greasy black and gray hairs on his scalp. I want to hunch down to his size, but I feel my father's stare and sit up straight and proud.

Uncle John touches my hand. His skin is cool and smooth as a mango. "Your father tells me you need braces. Is that so?"

I nod, recalling visits to the orthodontist, the X-rays and consultations, suggestions to push my front teeth up to the bone to eliminate the overbite that makes me look like Bugs Bunny. "Beaver Teeth," my classmates call me.

"And your sister, Cynthia, does she dance?"

I nod again, remembering her last performance in *Giselle*, how she fluttered across the stage dressed in a gossamer gown my mother had sewn.

"Is she any good?"

"She has talent. She's going to New York someday to be a prima ballerina."

"And you. What do you like to do?"

I wasn't expecting this question. I think for a minute. What's the right answer? "Read and draw."

"What do you draw?"

"Mostly people's faces. I like to capture their expressions."

"Could you capture me?"

I tilt my head, studying Uncle John in the harsh light. He seems small and frail, like a lab monkey who has suffered one too many experiments. "I could try," I say, "but I mostly draw women."

"Why women?"

"They're more fascinating."

"Really?" Uncle John leans back and clasps his hands between his knees. "Do you not find me fascinating?"

I shrug. Chee did not coach me in how to answer such a question.

Uncle John raises his eyebrows and shifts his body from side to side, as if modeling for an invisible camera. "How do you see me?" he asks.

"I don't know." The elastic waistband constricts my middle. I turn around, hoping to get some help from Chee, but he is standing at the other end of the room, pretending not to notice me.

Uncle John touches my arm. Again I am shocked that skin so dry and wrinkled can feel so smooth and cool. "What do you mean, you don't know?" he says.

Perspiration pastes the brown curls to my forehead. I tug on my waistband. I don't want to say anything without my father's approval. Already I feel I have said too much.

Uncle John's grip tightens on my forearm. "Answer me," he says.

"I can't."

"Why not?"

"Because . . ."

"Shall I tell your father you do not answer your elders when they speak?"

"I don't want to lie."

"Then tell me the truth. How do you see me?"

I stare into his brown-and-yellow eyes and the hard lines of his skin, pulled tight over his unforgiving cheekbones. I remember the last time we visited his house, how he left us with his sick wife after dinner so he could watch a basketball game.

"You're a mean old man."

"Mean?"

"You don't care about anyone except yourself."

"What makes you say that?" he asks.

And, without thinking of what my father would say, I tell him everything: "You didn't give my dad a job when he was laid off and couldn't find work. You hired a stranger instead, someone who stole money from you. You laughed when my mother had to get a job. I heard you tell Uncle Jimmy, 'American women like to bring home the bacon.' And when Elizabeth wouldn't hug you because you always smell like rotten fish, you told everyone, 'She's a spoiled brat, pure American, not an ounce of Chinese blood.' And when my father showed you my straight-A report card, you said, 'It's a shame she's not a boy.' How can you expect me to say nice things about you when all you do is ridicule us?"

I stand up, but Uncle John won't release my arm. He pulls me close, so close I smell his sour-milk breath. "You're right," he says. "I'm all those things. But your father, he is no better. And your mother, she did no right by marrying him. But you and your sisters, it is no fault of yours. You could not choose your parents." He reaches into his front pocket and withdraws a red envelope bulging with crisp hundred-dollar bills. "Here. Take this."

I feel my parents and my sisters watching, holding their breath. I push Uncle John's hand aside and twist my arm free. My bladder sloshes like an angry storm. "Keep it. I don't want it."

I tip over the chair and shove past relatives toward the restroom door. Inside, I wait in line for a stall. The soles of my shoes stick to the floors. The walls sweat with the stench of urine, disinfectant, and rodent killer. I clutch my stomach and rock back and forth on my heels. "Hurry, hurry, hurry," I moan.

Lammie Pie crashes through the door, seizes my wrist, and asks, "What happened?"

"He offered me money, but I wouldn't take it."

Lammie Pie frowns and shakes my arm. "How could you? You know we need that money."

Tears wet my eyes. I can see my mother's pain and disappointment through her anger, but I don't care anymore.

Lammie Pie leads me out of the restroom. She whispers to Chee, who says to me, "Go back and apologize immediately and ask for the money back. Tell him you didn't know what you were saying."

"But I *did* know what I was saying."

"We could end up homeless if you don't apologize to Uncle John. Now go talk to him. Say you're sorry, or you're walking home tonight."

"But we live two hours away."

I imagine him leaving me there without a nickel. I imagine huddling in an alley until the cops, or someone else, finds me. This isn't the first time Chee has threatened to make me walk home. The previous time was when I was five and couldn't count to one hundred. We were in the hospital parking lot waiting for my mother to finish with her doctor's appointment. Every time I got to thirty-two, I hit a blank spot. Chee opened the car door and yanked on my arm. "If you can't count to a hundred before your mom gets here, you're walking home."

I trembled. Cynthia stared at me with wide eyes. I tried to remember. Thirty, thirty-one, thirty-two . . . thirty-three. I did not have to walk home that day.

I gaze out the restaurant window. It is dark outside. I do not want to walk tonight. I tug on my skirt. "I need to go pee. Can I do that first?"

"No, he's leaving. Apologize and get the money, then you can go."

I sigh. Uncle John is helping Aunt Lil into a silk Chinese jacket embroidered with birds and fish.

"Uncle John?"

He turns. When he sees me, his frown blossoms into a smile. "Yes?"

"I'm sorry." The words feel like mothballs in my mouth.

He shakes his head. "No, you're right. I am a mean old man. But I can start over. I have a new life." He withdraws a red egg from the front pocket of his jacket and raises it like a gleaming coin.

I stare at the bulge in his other pocket, where the coveted envelope lies. "I should have taken the money. May I have it?"

"Why?"

"For my parents."

"What happened to your face?"

I touch my cheeks and wonder how long I have been crying.

Uncle John slips the red egg into his pocket and withdraws the envelope. He presses it against my palm, closing my fingers one at a time over the red paper. "Do not tell them what I'm going to tell you," he says. "I do not give this money to them, and I don't want your father asking for more. I am doing this for you, so you will think fondly of me when I am dead and will not tell your children I was a mean old man. Understand?"

I nod. My head swirls and my stomach tightens with cramps. I want to go to the restroom and then sleep on the drive home.

I clench the envelope in my fist and hug Uncle John. "Thank you," I say in Cantonese.

"Good luck." He kisses me.

Through the dissipating crowd, I see Chee standing with his feet apart, his coat folded over his crossed arms. He is waiting for me to bring the money that will sustain him for another few weeks. Elizabeth gazes sadly at me with her big brown eyes. I hand Chee the envelope, and he counts the bills. "Two thousand," he says to Lammie Pie who has just emerged from the restroom with Cynthia.

"I'll be right back." I catch the restroom door before it closes. "Will you wait for me?"

Chee nods, looking at the money in his hands.

In the restroom, I squeeze into a stall and relieve the ache in my bladder. My stomach still bulges beneath my dress, but it's no longer painful to breathe or move. I wash my hands with icy water and floral-smelling liquid soap. Cynthia and Elizabeth come in wearing their big snow jackets and ask, "Will you tell us a story?"

Their bodies are cut into jigsaw puzzles by the cracked mirror. I dry my wet hands with a rough paper towel. "What type of story?" I ask.

"A story about the moon," Cynthia says.

"A happy story," Elizabeth says.

With my left hand, I grasp Cynthia's; with my right, Elizabeth's. We step back into the restaurant. Lammie Pie smiles and nudges us toward the exit.

A brisk wind whips across my face. I pull my sisters close on either side and lean into a cold gust that smells of gasoline. We walk in tandem, left, right, left, right: a private march. Car engines throttle and roar. Brakes squeal. Relatives wave good-bye. We continue marching. Yellow-orange lights reflect off windshields. Dead leaves blow up around our ankles. Cynthia clutches her jacket against her throat, and Elizabeth looks up at the moonless sky. I listen to my mother's heels click against the concrete. My father links his arm in the crook of her elbow and asks, "Lammie, what should we do first?"

"Pay off the Visa," my mother says.

"But we need a new couch."

"The couch can wait. The bills come first."

Chee unlocks the van and slides the door open. We file inside and sit in the near darkness. Chee helps Lammie Pie up the step and closes the door. He starts the engine and turns on the headlights.

"I know," he says, leaning over to turn on the heat, "we'll go to Tahoe and double it."

3: DOUBLE OR NOTHING

The next morning, Chee shouts from the hallway, "Let's go!" I rub my eyes and blink. Morning shadows linger on my blue bedspread. I swing my feet over the side of the mattress and yawn.

"Did you call for a reservation?" Lammie Pie asks.

Chee drags a leather suitcase down the hall. He grunts as he lifts it onto the sofa. He unlatches the lock and begins to arrange underwear and socks around the perimeter of the suitcase.

I stand in the hallway gazing at my father. My mother hovers beside him with her arms crossed over her huge breasts.

"I don't want to drive down there and find out all the places are booked," she says.

"Not booked."

"How do you know?"

"Bill Harrah owes me a favor. He'll set us up in a good room at a good rate."

"In the middle of summer?"

Chee continues to pack.

Lammie Pie shrugs. "I guess we could always stay in the van."

"No van," Chee says. "I'll call." He shuffles down the hall past me and into his bedroom. He sits at his rolltop desk and dials the phone. I pretend I have to use the bathroom, but I leave the door open a crack so I can look and listen.

"Hello, Tracy. This is Dave Lam. I'm a friend of Bill Harrah. I want to book a room for tonight and tomorrow night. Two adults, three children. Really? May I speak with him? I know he can work something out. Oh, he's in Europe. On vacation. I see. When will he be back? Really? What can you do for me today?" Chee punches numbers into his calculator. The white tape burps and spits out the total in red ink. Chee lifts the tape and sighs. He hangs up the phone.

"You're right, Lammie Pie. No rooms."

"Well, why didn't you book something for later in the month? Isn't your vacation in a couple of weeks? We could go then."

I flush the toilet and run the water in the sink. I peek my head around the corner and glimpse Chee's surprised face. For a moment, he looks like he is going to speak, but then he picks up the phone. He dials again. "Hello, I was speaking with Tracy about booking a room this summer. What do you have available two weeks from now?"

The receptionist schedules us for the middle of the week at a discounted rate. That night, Chee asks if I'll play blackjack with him. "Just for ten minutes," he says, grabbing his poker chips and setting them on the kitchen table under the electric lights. I pull back a dining room chair and sit across from him. I take a red chip from the stack of chips Chee has given me and set it in the center of the table, announcing my bet. Chee deals three sets of cards, one for me, one for himself, and one for the invisible dealer.

My father has played blackjack with me since I was old enough to walk and talk. He taught me how to read the dealer's hand. "Small card means it's okay to take chances," Chee said. "You're hoping the dealer will keep hitting till he busts. A big card means trouble. Don't do anything risky. Just hold if you've got seventeen or higher, okay?" Chee showed me tricks he learned when he was a college student working summers at Harrah's as a blackjack dealer. "I was the best dealer in town," he explained with pride. "But I was also the best player. Bill knew that. He'd pay me double just so I would gamble at the other casinos. That's how we became good friends."

The closer we get to our trip to Tahoe, the more serious the games become. When Chee loses, he curses in Cantonese and says, "One more time."

It's only when Lammie Pie touches Chee's shoulder and says, "It's ten o'clock. Won't you let her get some rest?" that my father reluctantly acknowledges the time stops the game.

I play to keep my father company, not to win or lose. For me, it is not a game, not a strategy, but a time of quiet contemplation, a time when my father does not lecture me about the disappointments in life or scold me for my inadequacies. We sit across the table from each other like two adults in prayer. His intense focus reminds me of the dedication I pour into my studies, and for a while, I honor and respect him much more than at any other time.

"Twenty-one," he says with pride when I strike it lucky on the first turn. "You should have bet double."

"Then I would have lost," I say.

"That's no way to think," Chee says, gathering up the cards and tossing me the winning chips. "Half of winning starts here, in the mind." He taps the side of his forehead and smiles. "You think you win, you have better chance of winning. You think you lose, you might as well not play. Got it?"

I nod and bet two red chips instead of one.

Chee's fast moving hands deal another round. The dealer's hand exposes a seven. It could go either way, I think. I gingerly pick up my hand and sigh. Six and eight. Not good. I flip the bottom of my cards against the table, begging for a hit. Five. Better. I place my cards down and set my chips on top indicating I am done. Chee doubles down on two aces. He gets ten on one, five on the other. He flips over the dealer's hand. Ten. The dealer holds. I win. Chee wins one hand, loses the other. A smile flickers over his face. "Having fun?" he asks.

I nod and double my bet again.

Chee loses with a seven and ten. The dealer hits till he gets twenty. I tie.

We play again.

After a while, my eyes grow tired. My mind starts to wander. Without caring about the game anymore, I bet all my chips.

"Why you do that?" Chee asks.

"Because I want to go to bed."

"You could lose everything," Chee says.

I shrug.

Chee reluctantly deals the final hand. I set my cards on the table.
"Aiyaah!" Chee shouts. "Twenty-one!"

I smile.

"Look, Lammie Pie," Chee shouts. "Your daughter lucky! See
how she bets everything and wins!"

Lammie Pie hustles into the kitchen with needles sticking out of
her mouth from pinning a new pattern to the material she bought
last week on sale. She glances down at the table then up at me.

"See!" Chee shouts. "She win!"

Lammie Pie removes the needles from between her lips. "Too
bad you can't do that," she mumbles.

"Maybe we can sneak her in. Let her play a few hands."

Lammie Pie sniffs. "Yeah, right. Like security won't notice she's
underage."

"We put makeup on her, dress her in your clothes, let her wear
high heels. No one will know."

"Forget it," Lammie Pie says. "Let her go to bed. I want to finish
sewing."

Chee gathers me into his lap for a good-night kiss. His stubble
scratches my cheek. I wrap my arms around his neck and smell the
greasy Pomade perfume of his hair. He wraps his long arms around
me and presses me against his solid chest. His T-shirt reeks of perspiration. I peck his cheek and turn my face so he can plant his thick
lips against my skin. A smear of moist saliva wets my cheek, but I
don't wipe it away like my mother does. I carry it with me to bed. I
grab my rosary from my nightstand and pray till my eyes are heavy.
Then I tuck the rosary underneath my pillow and hug my radio
Chow dog and drift to sleep while listening to the latest adventure of
The Shadow on Old Time Radio Theater.

———

A week later, Chee asks us to pack for the trip. My sisters and I
follow orders. Our three suitcases line up along the back of the
van like toy soldiers. In our school backpacks, we stuff Mad Libs,
paperback novels, coloring books, and paper dolls for entertain-
ment during the drive. Cynthia packs her Sony Walkman. At

first, we try to read, but Chee wants to talk. "Look at that person driving and putting on makeup," he says, pointing to a woman in a compact car. "Don't do that when you learn to drive. Not safe. Use both hands on steering wheel." We put away our books and start to color, but Chee sways against the bumps dividing the lanes. Our hands jiggle. Crayon marks stray outside the lines. We sigh. As a last resort, we fold evening dresses around our paper dolls' shoulders. The dolls dance in circles like princesses at a ball. Chee glances into the rearview mirror and asks, "What are you doing?"

"Playing dolls," Elizabeth says.

"Aiyaah! Why don't you read?"

"We can't read when you're talking," Cynthia says.

Chee is quiet the rest of the trip.

———

At the hotel, Elizabeth strips and slips into her swimsuit. With a deft hand, she twirls her waist-length brown hair into a bun and tucks it into a blue rubber swim cap. Slipping into a pair of flip-flops, she grabs a towel from the rack in the bathroom.

Chee opens the door and asks, "Ready for dinner?"

He glances down at Elizabeth, who tries to squeeze past him. "Aiyaah! What you doing?" he asks.

Elizabeth drapes the towel over the crook of her arm and says, "Going swimming."

"Not now. Tomorrow," Chee says. "Time for dinner."

Chee counts the bills and coins in his pocket. "C'mon, get dressed, we go to all-you-can-eat buffet. If you don't like something, you don't have to eat it. You can get up and get something else, okay?"

Cynthia and I wait for Elizabeth to slip back into her T-shirt, shorts, socks, and tennis shoes.

In the elevator, Chee smiles at us. "Hope you're hungry."

At the entrance of the restaurant, we follow Chee's instructions and grab a tray and a plate and silverware wrapped in white cloth napkins. We slide our tray across the steel bar and fill our plates with salads, breads, steaming vegetables, pork, roast beef, and fried chicken. By the time we wind our way across the room, our plates are small mountains of food.

Chee helps us carry our trays to a table across from the dessert display. Cynthia's eyes widen. "Look at all that whipped cream," she whispers.

Elizabeth ogles the chocolate mousse and cheesecake and bite-sized éclairs. She walks over to the display and grabs another plate. Chee stalks over and slaps her wrist. "Eat dinner, first. Dessert later."

Elizabeth slinks back to the table and slides across the red vinyl bench seat and stares longingly at the fountain and ice sculptures in the center of the dessert display. She takes a few bites of her roast beef and salad, and nibbles on her warm bread roll. Cynthia shovels spoonful after spoonful of macaroni salad into her mouth and chews. A waiter stops to fill our water glasses. Cynthia smiles at him. Her eyes narrow into brown almond slits and her teeth flash. He smiles and bows slightly at her before turning to the next table.

"He likes you," I say.

Cynthia nods. "Every guy likes me."

Elizabeth fumes. "You can't have them all."

"Why not?" Cynthia asks.

"Because," Elizabeth reasons, "you couldn't possibly fit them all into your room."

Cynthia laughs.

"What's so funny?" Chee asks, returning from the buffet with a second plate of food.

"Nothing," Cynthia says, glancing down at her plate.

I notice Lammie Pie has not said anything. She gazes out the window with a faraway look on her face.

"What's wrong, Mom?" I ask.

She glances at me like I'm a stranger. She forces a smile. There are creases at the corners of her tired eyes. "Nothing," she says.

"Do you like the food?" Chee asks us.

We nod in unison.

Chewing a tender bit of roast beef, I glance around the dark room full of windows offering a panoramic view of the city and the mountains and the shimmering lake. Silky jazz saxophones whisper into my ears. Tiny white candles flicker from every table. The click of silverware and glasses mingles with people's low chatter. I survey the room, looking for a particular face to spark my imagination. I discover a woman with a coif of black hair and ruby-red lips nibbling on the edge of a croissant. Golden flakes flutter across the velvet bodice of her tight-fitting dress. My fingers itch for a pencil. I want to shade her high cheekbones with light and shadows. When she leaves the restaurant with her friends, I scan the room for another face. My gaze dances over people who pucker and chew and smile.

Cynthia nudges me with her elbow. "Ready for dessert?" she asks.

Already Elizabeth circles the dessert table. I push my chair back and stand up. I look down at my half-finished plate of roast beef, grilled chicken, green beans, potato salad, linguine, and bread, and wait for my father's approval. He nods. "Don't worry. You don't have to finish anything."

Cynthia squeezes my hand. "Want to take some back with us?" she asks.

"How?"

"Watch and learn." She leans over to a waiter who is replacing an empty platter with cherry-covered cheesecake. "Excuse me, sir, but I was wondering if I could have a take-out box."

He glances down at her. His long face breaks into a smile. "Sure. Wait here," he says.

Cynthia squeezes my elbow and giggles. "Works every time," she says.

"You've done this before?" I ask.

"At Bridget's birthday party I took home an entire pizza."

I raise my eyebrows, impressed by my sister's ingenuity and boldness.

In a few moments, the waiter returns with a white box. Cynthia winks and thanks him. He soaks in her radiant smile.

At the dessert table, I grab a small porcelain plate edged with gold and stack it full of truffles, a slice of chocolate mousse pie, miniature éclairs, and fresh strawberries and whipped cream. I return to the table and sit down with my treasure.

Cynthia fills a plate and sits down beside me.

"Where's the box?" I ask.

"I want to see what's best, first," she explains. "No use getting things I don't like."

I nod, understanding completely the logic behind her statement. Lammie Pie rises from the table and returns with a petite serving of chocolate mousse pie and nothing else. Chee shouts, "They have twenty different things to eat and that's all you choose?"

Lammie Pie gazes patiently at him. "I'm on a diet, remember? I have thirty-five pounds to lose. Don't you want me to look like those models in the magazines you're always showing Angela?"

Chee's face darkens with a furious anger. He tries to find a way around Lammie Pie's argument. "This once-in-a-lifetime experience," he says. "Don't pass up the opportunity. You diet when we get home, okay?"

Lammie Pie stares at him.

"Go, try everything, now!" he says.

Lammie Pie scoots from the table. A smug smile creases the corners of her thin lips. She returns with a plate stacked higher than any of our plates. Elizabeth and I exchange looks of amazement. Chee pats Lammie Pie's shoulder and proudly says, "That's the way to do it! Try everything!"

Chee starts to stand up, but reconsiders and taps Elizabeth on the shoulder. "You get me one of everything like Lammie Pie," he says.

Elizabeth stares at me. I nod. We circle the dessert table together, selecting everything except the chocolate desserts for Chee, who prefers fruits and whipped cream and pastries.

"Why'd he ask me to do it?" Elizabeth asks.

"Because he's too full to stand up and get it himself," I say.

She stares at me. "Really?"

I shrug. "Or he's lazy."

She smirks. "That's probably it."

We return with the plate of goodies. Chee glances at it, then at Lammie Pie's plate. "Aiyaah! You forgot that pie," he says, pointing to the slice of chocolate mousse Lammie Pie is eating.

I sigh. "I thought you didn't like chocolate."

"I don't. But I must try everything."

We grab another plate, but the chocolate mousse pie is gone. Cynthia comes up to us and asks, "What's the matter?"

"Dad asked for something they ran out of," I say.

Cynthia raises her hand and hails the waiter who gave her the white take-out box.

"Yes, ma'am," he says, bowing.

"Do you have more of that chocolate pie?" she asks. "I want to take some back to the room with me."

"Certainly." He whispers to another waiter, who disappears and returns with a new chocolate mousse pie on a silver platter.

Cynthia smiles at us. "Easy as pie," she says, giggling at her own joke.

We grab a slice and bring it back to Chee.

He lifts his fork and scoops up a mouthful. Chocolate smears over his lips.

"Not bad," he says. "But I like cherry cheesecake better."

We finish our desserts, push back our plates, and sigh with fullness.

"Ready to go?" Chee asks.

We nod in unison and follow him out of the dimly lit restaurant down the hall to the elevator. As it descends to our floor, Chee explains the itinerary for the night. "I'm going to play the tables while Lammie Pie gets you dressed and helps you say prayers, then she's going to come down and join me. If you need anything, call the front desk, okay?"

We nod again.

In the hotel room, Cynthia slips the white box under the double bed she and I will share. Elizabeth turns on the TV and flips through the channels. I slip into the bathroom to brush my teeth.

"You don't have to stay," I tell Lammie Pie. "I can take care of the girls."

"Are you sure?" she asks, furrowing her brows. I know she is worried about my father betting too much, too soon.

"I'm sure. I do it all the time at home." Which is true. Since she's returned to working part-time at the bank, I spend a couple of hours a day watching my sisters. How much harder could it be supervising them in a hotel room?

Lammie Pie surveys the room. My sisters sit quietly at the foot of their beds watching a commercial on TV. She glances down and kisses my forehead. "All right. Thanks. I'll be back before midnight with your father," she says.

She kisses my sisters good night and tells them to obey me while she's gone. Cynthia stares at her blankly. Elizabeth clutches her shirt and won't let go. "Please, stay," she says, "till we fall asleep."

"Angela will take care of you," she says. "She can tell you a story. Won't you, Angela?"

I nod, wondering if I have any energy left to conjure up something to sustain their attention in comparison to the flickering lights and sounds of the TV.

Elizabeth sniffs back a few tears and sidles over to me. She clutches the edges of my nightshirt and gazes up into my face. "Tell me a nice story," she says, "not a scary one."

I stroke her head and wonder what I can tell her. My head is full of scary, not nice, thoughts. My mother leaves. As soon as the door clicks shut, Cynthia turns up the volume on the TV.

"Go brush your teeth and change into your pj's," I tell Elizabeth. "Then I'll tell you a story."

———

Long after my sisters have fallen asleep listening to me tell of the romance between Sun and Moon, I am awakened by the click of the door. The digital clock on the nightstand glows 12:00 a.m. My parents' shuffling feet and murmuring voices fill the room. I tuck my hands under my cheek and pretend to be asleep.

"I didn't lose that much," Chee whispers.

"You didn't stop when I told you to," Lammie Pie hisses.

"Don't worry. I win it back tomorrow. Promise."

Lammie Pie shuts the bathroom door. Chee sits on the edge of the queen-size bed and removes his shoes. He reaches into his pocket and empties the contents on the bedspread. I close my eyes and drift back to sleep.

Later, in the midst of shadowy dreams, I roll over and open my eyes and glimpse my father's long shadow leave as the door clicks shut. My mother lies asleep in the bed beside me. The digital clock glows 3:30 a.m. For a moment, I consider stretching out my arm and touching my mother's soft curls and asking where Dad's going, but I decide to roll over and close my eyes.

Just as pink sunlight tickles the curtains, Lammie Pie wakes with a gasp. She shoves her thick hips into pants, pulls a shirt over her head, and steps into her shoes. I sit up.

"Did you hear anyone wake up in the middle of the night?" she asks.

I nod. "Dad. At 3:30."

My mother glances at the digital clock on the nightstand. 6:30 a.m. "Shit!" she says. Then, lowering her voice, she asks, "Can you watch your sisters? I need to go downstairs and find your father for breakfast."

I nod. "Is it that bad?" I ask.

My mother gazes at me sorrowfully and for a second I think she might confide the truth. But she holds firm to whatever it is she's thinking and says, "It'll be all right."

I clutch the rosary beads tucked under my pillow and rub my fingers over the crucifix.

"I'll be back as soon as possible," she says. "If your sisters wake, help them dress, okay?"

I nod and watch her go.

When the door clicks shut, I wander into the bathroom and turn on the light. I stare at my reflection and wonder if I look older from troubled sleep.

Returning to the room, I sit at the round table and pull out a pad of paper from the top bureau drawer. With the black ballpoint pen I find beside the telephone, I draw my sisters hunched beneath the blankets, their long eyelashes curled against their full cheeks, their tiny noses wriggling almost imperceptibly as they breathe, their triangular lips slightly parted, their small hands, and short, clean nails.

Cynthia turns away from my view. I start to sketch the back of her head, the dark, matted curls against the white sheets. Elizabeth yawns, stretches, and sits up, clutching Leppy. Her long brown hair cascades over her shoulders and down the front of her nightgown.

"What're you doing?" she asks.

"Drawing a picture of you," I say.

"May I see?"

I bring the notepad over to the rollaway bed. She gazes at her picture and asks, "Do I really look like that when I'm sleeping?"

I shrug. "It's just my impression," I say.

She stares at it intently. "I'm almost pretty," she says.

I smile. "No, you're absolutely beautiful!"

"Really?"

Cynthia props herself up on an elbow and squints at us. "What are you guys talking about?"

"Angela drew pictures of us. Want to see?"

Cynthia purses her lips and extends her arm. I slip the notepad into her hand. She studies the sketches. "Not bad," she says. "But my cheeks aren't that big."

"You rolled over before I was finished," I say.

She sighs. "I didn't know you were drawing me or I would have kept still."

"Where's Mom and Dad?" Elizabeth asks, glancing around the room.

"Mom went to tell Dad it's time for breakfast."

"He was gone all night?" Cynthia asks.

"Not all night. He came back once at midnight."

"Why'd he leave again?" Elizabeth asks.

"I don't know."

"Probably to gamble," Cynthia says.

Elizabeth pulls her knees to her chest and wraps her arms around her knees. "Are you sure they're coming back?" she asks.

I hear panic in her trembling voice. I try to reassure her, tell her they'll be back soon, but she just huddles on the bed. Tears roll down her cheeks. "They've left us," she sobs.

"Stop crying," Cynthia says, getting out of bed. "Didn't you hear anything Angela said? They're coming back for breakfast."

"How do you know for sure?" Elizabeth sniffs.

"It's easy, stupid. Dad loves food more than he loves money."
Cynthia kneels beside the bed and withdraws the white take-out
box. "Want a truffle?"

Elizabeth reaches for a square of chocolate decorated with a pink
rose.

"You guys will spoil your appetite," I remind them. "I told Mom
I'd have you dressed and ready before they got back."

"But they could be gone all day," Elizabeth says, licking pink
frosting from her upper lip.

The lock turns and the door swings open. Cynthia and Elizabeth
swallow their goodies and scramble beneath the covers, pretending
to be asleep. I stand up and walk across the room.

Chee and Lammie Pie are arguing, but stop as soon as they see
me. "Ready to eat?" Chee asks, all smiles.

"Looks like they're still sleeping," Lammie Pie says. "Maybe we
should get them up. It's almost eight."

I go over and pretend to shake my sisters awake. They rub their
eyes, yawn, stretch, and pretend to be sleepy.

"Hurry up! Dress! We're leaving in ten minutes," Chee says.

My sisters scramble out of bed and into the bathroom. Minutes
later, they're wearing red blouses and jeans, and their permed hair
is fluffed and combed.

We follow Chee and Lammie Pie into the elevator to the first
floor. We pass people playing blackjack and slot machines. Cocktail
waitresses in glittering beaded leotards and glossy tights serve
drinks. I hook a finger through a loop in Chee's pants and motion
for my sisters to grab a hold of each other. We snake through the
lobby, quiet in a sea of whirrs and hisses, clicks and rattles. By the
time we reach the breakfast café, we are wide-eyed and breathless.

Chee follows a waiter to a leather booth and we slide across the
seat facing him and Lammie Pie. We open our menus and spy a photo
of a chocolate pancake with a whipped cream smile and cherry nose
and eyes. We decide to order that. "No eggs?" Chee asks us.

We shake our heads in unison and fold our menus on the table.

Numbers flash on a television screen above our heads. Chee
grabs a piece of paper and pencil from behind the napkin holder

and scribbles some numbers down. His dark face is animated and tense at the same time.

"What are you doing?" I ask.

"Playing Keno," he explains.

Before I have a chance to ask what Keno is, a waitress with a blonde ponytail arrives to take our order. She winks at Elizabeth and jots down our requests. Chee hands her his Keno ticket and five dollars.

"If I win, you'll get a bigger tip," he says, smiling.

After the waitress leaves, Lammie Pie leans over to Chee and whispers, "If you win, we're going home."

Chee nods.

My sisters and I swing our legs under the table. Around the room people bend over steak and eggs and pancakes doused with warm maple syrup. The air smells of smoke, coffee, and grease. For a moment, no one speaks.

Chee watches the screen, studying the ticket receipt the waitress handed him. His facial expression never changes.

When the screen clears and another game begins, Lammie Pie nudges him. "We're leaving," she says.

Elizabeth's eyes widen. "But you promised we'd go swimming!"

Lammie Pie sighs with relief. She reaches across the table and pats Elizabeth's hand. "Next time."

Without waiting for our breakfasts to arrive, Lammie Pie uncurls a twenty-dollar bill, tosses it on the table, and escorts us to the van. She returns to the hotel with Chee to collect his winnings and pack our suitcases.

Wow! I think. *I wonder how much he won.*

In the van, my sisters and I strap seatbelts tightly over our laps. Chee shifts the van into gear and swerves recklessly over the curb. He weaves through traffic, speeding through yellow lights before they turn red.

"I want to go swimming," Elizabeth says.

"Next time," Chee replies.

My stomach grumbles. "I'm hungry. When are we going to get breakfast?"

"Later," Chee says. "Once we cross over to California."

Cynthia nudges my arm and winks. "You should have eaten a truffle."

I wrap my arms around my waist and narrow my eyes at her.

For a while, no one says anything. I try not to think about the hot chocolate pancake with whipped-cream eyes and a cherry nose and lots of warm maple syrup I would be eating if Chee hadn't won Keno. Buildings fall away and trees sprout up along the ridge of the mountain. Light and shadows flicker over us. Chee eases up on the gas after we descend the first mountain.

Elizabeth's voice shakes with tears and anger. "You promised we'd go swimming!"

"Next time," Chee repeats.

"No, right now," Elizabeth says.

Lammie Pie glances over her shoulder and says, "Calm down. There's been an emergency. We have to go home."

"What kind of emergency?" Elizabeth asks in a trembling voice.

"Grandma and Grandpa need us," Chee says.

"Why didn't they call Aunt Mildred like they always do?" Elizabeth asks. Then, as the trees fall away and the road opens to the freeway, Elizabeth sniffs. "How do you know they need you? No one called us."

"They left a message at the front desk. That's why I had to leave before breakfast," Chee explains.

"You're lying to me." Elizabeth folds her arms over her chest and stares out the window. "I'm never believing you again."

My empty stomach groans. I know if I offer to comfort Elizabeth, I will start crying too, but for different reasons. She wanted to swim. I wanted to eat.

Cynthia taps my arm. "Do you still have Mad Libs?" she asks.

I reach into the pocket behind Lammie Pie's seat and remove the booklets and a pen. I flip through the pages and ask, "Which one do you want to do? My Summer Vacation or Back to School?"

"Back to School," Cynthia says. "I already know how My Summer Vacation ends."

4: SURPRISE

I stare out the tinted windows of the van. Already we have left the Sierra Nevadas. The trees and rivers and mountains have given way to gray concrete and more and more cars. The freeway sign reads SAN JOSE 110 MILES.

Chee and Lammie Pie are oddly silent. When I close my eyes, I can hear the whoosh of passing trucks and the tinny drums from Cynthia's headphones.

I am jostled awake by the booming sound of Chee's voice.

"Hey, girls," he says. "Want to go to Disneyland?"

"Yeah!" Cynthia says, removing her headphones.

Elizabeth sits up and rubs her eyes. "I don't believe you," she says.

"No, it's for real," Chee says. "Tell them I'm not lying, Lammie."

My mother glances back at us and repeats what Chee has already said. "He's not lying," she adds, as if to convince us.

Elizabeth crosses her arms over her chest and squints. "I'll believe it when I see Sleeping Beauty's castle," she says.

"When are we going?" Cynthia asks.

"As soon as we get home, wash our clothes, and pack again," Chee says, glancing at us in the rearview mirror. "I just have to make a few quick calls to get us a room, okay?"

"What about Grandpa and Grandma?" Elizabeth asks.

"What about them?" Chee asks.

"Don't they need us? Isn't that why we're going back?" Elizabeth asks.

Chee is silent. He glances at Lammie Pie, hoping for some direction.

"Your dad lied," Lammie Pie says. "Grandpa and Grandma didn't call. We won money and we didn't want to lose it. So we left early."

Elizabeth wails. "I *knew* it! We could have gone swimming. I knew you lied to me!"

"He lied to *all* of us," Cynthia reminds her. "Not just you."

"And he's lying about Disneyland."

"No, I'm not," Chee says. "Lammie Pie, tell them."

My mother puts her cross-stitch in a white plastic bag and shifts in her seat to face us. Her blue eyes are bright and her cheeks are flushed. "Your father lost a lot of money last night and so he tried to make up for it this morning—"

"And I did!"

Lammie Pie frowns at Chee. "Don't interrupt or I'll let you do the explaining."

"Oh, all right."

Lammie Pie waits for a moment before she continues. "So this morning, your dad played Keno. And he won the grand prize."

"How much?" I ask.

Chee taps the steering wheel in an imitation drum roll. "Twenty-five thousand dollars!"

"Really?" I ask.

Chee nods. "Your mom is good luck. She comes and watches me play. If I'm winning, she takes the chips and cashes them in. If I'm losing, she tells me to stop for a while. We work well as a team. Just like you and your sisters, when you put your minds to it."

"How long will we be gone?" I ask.

"Five days," Chee says. "Almost a week. Is that good enough?"

"I don't care how long we stay," Elizabeth says, "as long as we go swimming."

When we get home, we launder our clothes and pack again. We leave early the next morning, stopping briefly at Winchell's for a dozen donuts. We eat while Chee drives. The road to Anaheim is straight and narrow with fields of artichokes and corn on either side. Chee has brought the portable toilet. He wedged it between the driver's seat and Cynthia's seat. Whenever one of us has to go, Cynthia slips into the back of the van and pitches her nose. "Why don't we just stop?" she asks Chee.

"Do you want to get there tonight or tomorrow?" Chee asks.

In Bakersfield, we pull up to a Burger King drive-through and order hamburgers, fries, and sodas. We eat in silence and stare out our windows as Chee pulls back onto the freeway. After we eat, we play cards, color in our Barbie coloring books, and nap.

We reach the Disneyland Hotel in the early evening. Our room overlooks the Never Land Pool where children climb a mountain trail, cross a suspension bridge, and slide down a waterslide into the deep water. Elizabeth slips into her bathing suit and flip-flops and grabs a towel.

"Not yet," Chee says.

"Yes, right now."

Chee purses his lips.

"You promised. Remember?" Elizabeth says. Tears well up in her large brown eyes.

Lammie Pie slips into her bathing suit and flip-flops and says, "We need a little exercise after sitting all day. And it's better to swim on an empty stomach."

Chee reluctantly nods. Cynthia and I get dressed and wait for Chee to grab some extra towels at the front desk. We pad across the winding cement paths past a peaceful oasis of tropical foliage, beautiful waterfalls, large ponds, and caves to the Never Land Pool. Elizabeth tosses her towel over a beach chair and dives into the water. Her long hair whips around her face as her body shoots through the water. She floats on her back, staring up at the palm trees and the brilliant orange and purple sky. Cynthia wades into the shallow end of the pool. She sits on a step and kicks her feet. I walk out into the water and watch Elizabeth paddle across the length of the pool like a steam engine.

"Hey," Chee says, a half hour later. "We can eat here. They have lots of restaurants."

We grab our towels and return to our room to shower and change. We follow Chee through a maze of trees, across a bridge, and past a waterfall to an open and airy thatched hut with women dressed in grass skirts and bikini tops. Chee wiggles through the loud, chattering crowd to the bar and orders five Planter's Punch Tahitian drinks and hands them to us. "Like Shirley Temples," he says. "Just juice." We take our orange-yellow drinks, searching for a place to sit down.

But there is standing room only. In an outside pavilion, a drummer hammers out an intense rhythm that vibrates through our chests. We sip our drinks and wedge our way through thighs to the edge of the bar where tiki lamps flare crimson and gold. Chee stands near a tall blonde with a bikini top of jungle leaves and pink flowers, and a frayed grass skirt the color of old hay. He smiles and laughs as he nudges her. She blushes under the deep tan of her skin and lowers her eyelashes, leaning closer to him so his mouth brushes against the tangle of her yellow hair when he whispers in her ear. He takes a piece of paper from his pocket and hands it to her, and she scribbles something down.

Lammie Pie sets her drink down and stampedes through the crowd and out of the bar. Cynthia and Elizabeth follow her, clutching their drinks to their chests like torches. I glance at Chee, then trail after my sisters as they weave through the tangle of smoke and elbows and knees.

Lammie Pie's short, thick legs jiggle inside the sky-blue polyester pants as she walks along the path to the hotel room. Her sandals slap against pavement. Cynthia hustles up to her and tries to hold her hand, but Lammie Pie shoves her aside.

I catch up to Elizabeth. We follow Lammie Pie to a bench beneath a palm tree. She sits down and sobs into her hands. Cynthia sets her drink under the bench and tries to wrap her arms around Lammie Pie, but she nudges her away.

Cynthia slumps down beside her and asks, "What's wrong?"

Lammie Pie lifts her head and opens her mouth to explain, but Chee hustles over to us in a fake jog, his arms pumping vigorously back and forth while his feet scuff and shuffle. "Aiyaah! I thought I lost you. Why you leave without telling me?"

"I had to chase the kids," Lammie Pie lies.

Chee glances at us and nods. "You stay with us next time," he says. "Don't make your mother cry." Then, to Lammie Pie, he asks, "Why didn't you get me?"

"You were too busy talking to that blonde," Lammie Pie says.

"She's a model with *Vogue*," he explains. "I got the name of her agent so we can have Angela model for them."

Lammie Pie glances at me and her eyes narrow with hateful venom.

I step back, suddenly afraid, and almost slip into the pond. My drink splashes. An orange puddle spreads across the pavement like a blooming bruise.

"Did you get the number?" Lammie Pie asks Chee.

"Yes, right here," he says, patting the pocket of his Hawaiian shirt. "I call after vacation. Aren't you hungry? Let's go to dinner."

Chee grabs Elizabeth's hand and my hand and starts down the path, but Lammie Pie and Cynthia remain sitting on the bench.

Chee glances back. He drags us by the arm toward Lammie Pie.

"What's wrong?" Chee asks.

Lammie Pie's blue eyes shimmer with tears. She glares at Chee and her cheeks tighten around her lips. "There's no agency."

"Yes, there is. Here's the number." He takes it out and shows her.

"How do I know it's not her home number instead?"

"Why would I want that?" Chee demands. "I have you."

"She's younger."

"You're young."

"And prettier."

"You're pretty."

"And thinner!"

Chee purses his lips and looks away.

"It's true," Lammie Pie says. The words sting more than the sharpness in her voice.

"I'll show you!" Lammie Pie declares. "I'll lose all this weight. And when I do, men will come after *me*."

"I wasn't going after her," Chee explains, but his words dissolve before they reach Lammie Pie's ears.

Elizabeth tugs Chee's arm. "I'm hungry!"

"Let's eat," Cynthia says, her hand on Lammie Pie's arm.

We walk in silence to the next restaurant. Tinkling music floats across the carpeted floor and out the open windows. When it is our turn to order, Lammie Pie requests the house salad with honey-lemon dressing on the side. During dinner, she refuses to try any of the foods we offer her. Instead, she sips iced tea and sizes up the waitresses as they pass our table.

I stare at my mother, at her sad face, at her angry eyes, and wonder if this is what it means to be a woman—an endless beauty competition in which the winner gets the attention of the desired man and the loser gets heartache and sorrow. My gaze travels across the room and pauses at all the women: some pretty, others not, some with men, others alone or with other women, some laughing, others staring at their food or smiling at their company. My mother eats in silence, nibbling her salad, sipping her iced tea, and marking out her territory with her fierce gaze directed at any woman who dares to glance in our direction.

I think of the fairy tales I have been told, of the fairy-tale place where we are, and I begin to question whether or not a happily-ever-after truly exists for the woman whose beauty wins the kiss.

5: The Right Doll

The next day after breakfast, we board the monorail to Disneyland. We are dropped off in Tomorrowland. Chee points to the right where the submarines dive into a lagoon. "Let's start here," he says.

When the ride is over, we wait for Chee to tell us where to go next. "Aiyaah!" he says. "How about that mountain over there?"

He points to the Matterhorn. We walk hand in hand to the big snow-capped mountain and stand in a long line beneath speakers pumping out recorded yodeling. Passengers shout as the bobsleds click-clack through hairpin turns.

"I don't think I want to go on this one," I say.

"Why not?" Elizabeth asks.

"Scaredy cat," Cynthia says.

"It's okay," Elizabeth says, squeezing my hand. "I'll protect you."

I smile in spite of myself. By the time we reach the bobsleds, my feet ache. I slide into the seat behind Elizabeth and grab the handles. I rest my back against the vinyl seat and take a deep breath as the bobsled ascends the steep rickety track. The first plunge jolts my stomach into my chest, and I swoon with fear. My palms sweat against the steel bars, but I manage to retain my tight grip through quick dips and sharp turns. The bobsled shoots out of the mountain, down a ramp, and splashes into a pool of water before rounding back to the start of the ride. My rapid breathing matches my heart rate.

Elizabeth springs out of the bobsled and jumps up and down shout-ing, "Can we do it again!" I climb out slowly, trembling and sweaty.

"Line's too long," Chee says. "Let's watch the parade."

We stand behind the rope. Chee takes out his camera and prac-tices aiming the lens at the walkway. Lammie Pie grabs Cynthia's hand and says, "The girls and I will be back in a few minutes. We're going to look in the shops by the castle."

We leave Chee and walk across the path to Sleeping Beauty's castle. We amble into Tinker Bell's gift shop. Cynthia spies a Snow White doll dressed in her blue-and-yellow dress with a red cape. "Oh, Mommy, may I have her, pleeease!" she begs, clutching the box to her chest.

Lammie Pie glances at the price, $32.99, and nods.

"What can I get?" Elizabeth asks. She searches up and down the shelves and across the rows, but cannot find anything she wants. At a turning display stand, she finds packets of Winnie-the-Pooh stick-ers. "I think I'll get these," she says, handing them to Lammie Pie.

"What about you, Angela?" she asks.

I gaze at the Cinderella doll. "It's just like the movie," Lammie Pie says, examining the doll. "Look. You can even change her into her party dress."

"That's not the dress I want," I say, matter-of-factly. "I want the ball gown the fairy godmother gave her."

Lammie Pie places the box back on the shelf. She glances around and finds another Cinderella doll dressed in the gown the fairy god-mother gave her. "Here," she says, handing it to me.

I frown at the pink dress and sigh. "She's wearing silver in the movie, not pink."

"Well, the Cinderella in the parade is wearing blue," she says, pointing to the picture in the brochure.

"But this is not blue," I protest. "It's pink." I don't know how to tell my mother I absolutely hate the ultra-feminine color. I want a Cinderella doll in a sky-blue or silver dress. Nothing else will do.

"Well, I guess we'll keep looking," Lammie Pie says. "There are plenty of shops here."

I sulk beside the counter as Lammie Pie pays for my sisters' goodies. Cynthia clutches her bag and sings, "Heigh-ho, heigh-ho, it's home from work we go," and lifts her feet in an exaggerated march. Elizabeth swings her slim bag of stickers. "Your total came to three dollars," Lammie Pie tells Elizabeth, "so you can get something else, too. Just let me know, okay?"

We wander back through the gathering crowd to the Matterhorn. Chee has moved in front of the rope. He smiles and waves his arms. The camera dangles around his neck.

Trumpets blare and music pipes through loud speakers strung overhead. "Welcome to the Magic Kingdom," the announcer says. "Enjoy the parade."

Chee aims his camera at the characters waltzing down the path. Halfway through the parade, I tug on Chee's shirt.

He leans down and I shout, "Can you get a picture of Cinderella?"

"Who's Cinderella?"

I point toward the blonde dressed in a glittering sky-blue ball gown dancing beside her fairy godmother and the mice.

Chee raises the camera to his eye and squints through the lens. He clicks the shutter again and again. I clap my hands and shout, "Thank you, Dad."

"Oh, I'm not done," he says, smiling down at me. "Just you wait." Chee yells, "Hey, Cinderella! Over here! Look over here!"

Cinderella twirls around and waves at the crowd. When she hears Chee's voice, she glances over her shoulder, but continues to dance.

"Hey, Cinderella! You're so beautiful! My daughter wants to be just like you when she grows up!"

Cinderella gazes at Chee and winks.

"That's it," Chee says, finishing the roll of film. "I got a good one for you, Angela. Up close and smiling. Just like she's dancing just for you."

I pat his back and smile. "Thanks again, Dad."

———

After the parade, we board the Monorail and head back to the hotel. Elizabeth places her stickers in the desk drawer, but Chee slaps her wrist. "Aiyaah! You forget and leave it here. Put in suitcase," he says.

Cynthia wedges the doll box into the center of her suitcase with her T-shirts, shorts, and underwear packed around it.

Elizabeth slips the stickers into the inside pouch where she stores her socks.

"What you get?" Chee asks me.

"Nothing," I say.

"Why not? You get straight A's in school. You clean the house. You teach your sisters. You deserve something most of all."

Lammie Pie stands at the bureau mirror and fluffs her golden brown hair with a pick. "She wants a Cinderella doll, but the shop didn't have the right kind."

Chee frowns. "What do you mean?"

"She was wearing the wrong color dress," I explain. "She's supposed to be wearing blue and silver, not pink and white."

"What's the difference?" Chee asks. "A doll is a doll."

I hold my breath and clench my fists gazing imploringly at my sisters, hoping one of them can translate what I just said.

Cynthia sits back on her heels beside her suitcase. In a loud, slow voice, she enunciates, "Pink is not blue."

"I know that," Chee says, sitting on the edge of the bed.

"What's the point of getting a doll that is wearing an incorrect outfit?" I say. "We're at Disneyland. They're supposed to know what their own characters are wearing!"

"Don't shout," Lammie Pie says.

I didn't know I was shouting.

Chee flexes his feet and studies the carpet. "We'll get you the right doll," he says. "I promise."

———

We return to the park after lunch. By the time we wander through Adventureland and Main Street USA, our feet are sore and our shoulders are sunburned. We slump against a bench and fan ourselves with brochures.

"Should we go back to the hotel?" Chee asks.

"What about shopping?" I ask, remembering my Cinderella doll.

"We can come back tomorrow and shop," Chee says.

"But we'll have to pay for another ticket."

"Angela's right," Lammie Pie says. "We should shop now."

We wander through gift shop after gift shop, but we don't find the right Cinderella doll.

"Why don't you buy this one?" Chee asks, handing me the doll dressed in rags. Her pink party dress glistens beside her.

I shake my head. My voice quivers. "I'd rather not get anything at all."

"Don't cry," Chee demands, placing the doll back on the shelf. "It's not my fault this time. I haven't broken my promise to you. We've gone through every shop in the park." His shoulders sag in defeat. "There's nothing else I can do."

"Yes, there is," Lammie Pie says, in a hopeful voice. "We can check the shops at the hotel."

Chee's face brightens. "Yes, that's it! We'll do it first thing tomorrow. After breakfast."

The next morning, Chee and I wander through the maze of paths to the gift shops. In Tinker Bell's Treasures, behind the counter, we spy a two-foot Cinderella doll in a white-and-blue ball gown. "That's it," I say, tugging on Chee's shirt.

He grunts, "Where?" and I point to the doll. "How much?" he asks the clerk.

The short man wearing a white jacket and black slacks stands on a stepladder and lifts the doll's dress. "Three fifty," he says.

"Three dollars and fifty cents?"

The man shakes his head. "Three hundred and fifty dollars."

"Three hundred and fifty dollars?" Chee repeats.

Lammie Pie enters the shop followed by Cynthia and Elizabeth. She sees the Cinderella doll standing behind the counter above the clerk's head. "You've found her," she says, smiling.

"For three hundred and fifty dollars," Chee says.

"Why so much?" Lammie Pie asks the clerk.

"She's porcelain," he states matter-of-factly. "And those are real pearls in her ears and real glass slippers."

The clerk takes her down from the shelf and lets me hold her. She's as heavy as the old dolls my mother has from when she was a child. Her eyes are a haunting blue, clear and deep like the ocean. She's big and clumsy, but she's wearing the right dress.

"Look," Lammie Pie says. "The tag says she has real hair and her eyes are genuine Australian crystals."

Chee purses his lips and thinks. "That's a lot of money for a doll."

Lammie Pie nods, fluffing the ruffle of the dress and admiring the stitching.

"How much did you spend on the girls?" Chee asks.

Lammie Pie shrugs. "Thirty dollars or so for Snow White and three dollars on stickers."

"Not a hundred dollars for a doll?"

Lammie Pie shakes her head. "But Snow White isn't as pretty as this."

I stare at Cinderella's face, her perfectly coiffed hair, her blue-and-white satin dress, her glittering glass slippers. My chest grows tight. It's hard to breathe.

"I can't buy it," Chee says, at last.

"Why not?" I ask, clutching the doll's thick porcelain legs.

"Too much."

Cynthia strolls over to the counter and examines the doll in my hands.

"That's as much as the Siamese cat Elizabeth wanted in San Francisco," she reminds us. "And Dad didn't buy it. Why should he buy you Cinderella?"

Chee looks down at her and says, "Angela does much more work than you do around the house. She gets good grades and never talks back. She deserves more than you." He gazes at me with his large brown eyes and he suddenly looks like Elizabeth when she is about to cry. "But this doll. It's too much."

I hand Cinderella back to the clerk and stalk out of the store and into the fresh air. The tightness in my chest loosens, but my throat constricts. I sniff and reach into my pocket for a tissue before Chee and the others come for me.

"I'm sorry," Chee says, grabbing my hand.

His skin is smooth and dry. I want to shake my hand loose, but his grip tightens. He gazes at me and I realize there are tears in his eyes.

"If I had more money," he says, trying to explain. "I would buy the doll."

If the clerk wasn't looking and there weren't security cameras everywhere, you would steal it, I think. I remember all the other times he has stolen things for us: Barbie dolls, clothing, even packs of gum. It's not because we're poor—I've seen my father's books and there's a little extra money, not much, but enough for a special buy every now and then—it's because he doesn't know how to say, "No." He doesn't know how to let us down without letting himself down. That's why there are tears in his eyes. This doll means as much to him as it does to me because I am his daughter and he wants me to be happy, even if it means breaking all the rules.

"I love you," Chee says, trying to reassure me.

"I know," I say, in a weak whisper.

"Good." He squeezes my hand one last time before he lets it go.

6: SHOW BIZ

efore leaving Anaheim, Chee suggests we eat a hearty breakfast. "Don't know when we'll get lunch," he says, opening the menu. Cynthia, Elizabeth, and I lean against the high-back seats of an American diner and order a menagerie of scrambled eggs, toast, English muffins, pancakes, bacon, and sausages. Whatever we can't eat, Chee finishes. Lammie Pie orders a fruit salad. Throughout our trip, she has refused to indulge in anything other than fruits and salads, egg whites and dried toast, roasted chicken and steamed vegetables. Although none of us has noticed any change in her weight, there seems to be a peaceful determination about her.

"We should have bought a camper," Lammie Pie says.

"Why?" Chee asks, before shoveling the rest of the scrambled eggs into his mouth.

"We could save a lot of time and money with a shower and a stove."

"Why stove?"

"These meals are expensive."

"Why cook? That's no vacation." Chee opens two containers of half-and-half and dumps them into his iced water and stirs it with a spoon.

Elizabeth points to the cloudy water. "What are you doing?"

"Making milk." Chee gulps the fluid down and smacks his lips. "Ahh! That hit the spot."

"If you're not worried about money, then why are you drinking creamer instead of real milk?" Lammie Pie asks.

Chee furrows his brow, crosses his arms on the table, and glances at the waitress who brings the tab. He instantly smiles, pulling out his wallet, and counting out the bills into the waitress's hand. "One for your mother, one for your sister, and one for you."

"Thanks," she says, pocketing the bills and clearing the plates.

After visiting the restroom one last time, we pack into the van and brace ourselves for our next destination.

"Where are we going?" Cynthia asks.

Chee thinks for a moment. "Home," he says.

"Home?" asks Elizabeth.

"If we didn't have bills to pay, we could go everywhere," Chee explains, glancing in the rearview mirror. "We'd see Johnny Carson on the *Tonight Show* and the Hollywood Walk of Fame. We'd see the wax museum and Knott's Berry Farm. We'd stop at Hearst's Castle." The tires thump against the yellow safety bumps, and Chee veers toward the center of the lane.

Lammie Pie slaps his shoulder. "Watch it or you'll get us all killed!"

"I drive okay," Chee says.

"You drive like a drunk," Lammie Pie scolds. "Stop talking and watch the road."

"They asked a question. I had to answer."

"They'll understand. Just drive."

A patch of silence follows. My sisters and I gaze out the tinted windows at people roller-skating on sidewalks lined with palm trees. At an intersection, a policeman waves us to the right. The road has been blocked off. Chee points to the left and says, "Look! Movie stars."

We peer out the window. People walk up and down a set of steps outside what looks like a courthouse. Cameras surround the scene. The director shouts into a white megaphone. When no one listens, he waves his hands overhead until the action stops. Makeup artists rush to the two main characters and dab their faces with tiny sponges. The crew gathers for a moment, listening intently to the director's words, before resuming their places.

The policeman raps against the driver's window and Chee rolls it down.

"Move along," the policeman says, "or I'll have to cite you."

"Okay, officer," he says, smiling. "My daughters just want to see a movie star, that's all."

"If you go to Universal Studios, you can see all the stars you want," the policeman says. "You can learn how they make movies and maybe star in one yourself."

"Really?" Chee leans closer, suddenly interested.

The policeman gives him directions and Chee thanks him with a five-dollar bill, but the policeman shakes his head and waves him away. "Go have fun," he tells Chee. "Enjoy your daughters. They grow so fast. My kids are in college already."

Chee turns to Lammie Pie. "Did you get the directions written down?" he asks.

"Keep driving. I'll tell you where to turn," she says.

Chee glances in the rearview mirror and asks, "Did you know I made a movie in college?"

Cynthia snickers. "Just like you made a record?"

There is an old forty-five of Chee singing "Love Me Tender" and "Blue Moon" that Lammie Pie sometimes plays whenever she's reminiscing about the days before she had children. Over the years, Chee's voice has faded and skipped in the recording. We giggle whenever we hear the low mumbling voice burst into a wave of bubbling sound before it simmers into a whimper and dies away. If we didn't know any better, we would have thought it was a ghost trying to scare us, not our father's sultry voice serenading our mother.

"No, I paid to make the record," he explains. "It was a present for Mah-Mah, but she didn't like it so I gave it to Lammie Pie. But I got paid to be in a movie." At a red light, he tilts his hip, removes his wallet, and flips through the plastic picture sleeves until he finds what he is looking for and hands it to me. "Show your sisters," he says.

It's a laminated card with a black-and-white photo of Chee's head and shoulders. The small type reads, Expires in 1965.

"What is it?" Cynthia asks.

"My Screen Actors Guild card," he says proudly.

At the next red light, Chee extends his arm back and wiggles his fingers, indicating he wants his wallet returned. I fold it up and place it in his palm. He slips it into his back pocket and says, "They were filming at University of Pacific. A war movie. The director told the campus president he wanted all former military officers to appear for a screen test. I passed." Chee flashes an ivory smile into the rearview mirror. "We had to play soldiers in a war. We rehearsed for ten hours a day."

"What movie?" Cynthia asks.

"I forget the name," he says. "It's so long ago. But maybe Lammie Pie remembers."

"I don't watch war movies," she says, "and besides, this happened long before I met you."

Chee pauses, as if trying to remember where one life left off and another life began.

"Anyway," Chee says, "we filmed for two weeks. They wanted me to say a few lines, but I kept stuttering, so they picked the guy next to me to say them instead. I remember standing shoulder to shoulder with him, hoping for a close-up. When the film was released a year later, they had cut the scene out completely. I watched the movie three times to make sure, but I didn't see myself anywhere. It was a waste of time."

"But you got paid?" Cynthia asks.

"Yes, but not much. Only minimum wage because I didn't have a Screen Actors Guild card. I got the card after making the movie, but then I didn't act again."

"Why not?" I ask.

"No more movies wanting Chinamen," he explains.

"Why not?"

Chee shrugs.

"Why'd they want you in the first place?" Cynthia asks.

"It was about the Korean War."

"Why didn't they cast Koreans?"

"Not enough of them in San Francisco. Mostly Chinese. They

took everyone they could get with slanted eyes," Chee explains. "That's show biz."

We glance at each other, wondering which movie Chee starred in for two weeks before getting every one of his scenes left on the cutting room floor.

A half hour later, we arrive at Universal Studios. I hold my sisters' hands and we walk to the entrance where Chee stands in line to buy tickets. The sun's warmth feels like a hand against my back. I smile at the crowds of people milling about the entrance and wonder who they are and where they come from.

"Excuse me," someone says.

I glance over my shoulder. A man who looks to be my father's age smiles at me. He adjusts a white cap on his head of thick brown hair, and I notice a ribbon of sweat gleaming on his forehead.

He leans forward until he is eye level with me. "Would you mind doing a screen test?" he asks.

I lift my eyebrows and point to my chest.

He nods and smiles. "Yes, you."

I start to follow the stranger, but Chee nudges me back into the line. "What you doing?" The question is directed at me, but his gaze is directed at the stranger.

"Sir, is this your daughter?"

Chee wraps a protective arm around my shoulders and pulls me close. "Yes, she is my first born. These two are also mine." He points to Cynthia and Elizabeth, who squint at the stranger.

"I don't want to harm any of your beautiful daughters," the stranger says. "I just want to know if your oldest here can act in a screen test?"

When Chee frowns, the stranger points behind him to the cameraman, who waves at us. There, a few feet from the parking lot, is a makeshift set with a neutral background and a video camera propped on a tripod. A floodlight beams under the protective embrace of a silver umbrella.

Chee's face breaks into a smile. He nudges me toward the stranger. "Do it! Be a movie star. Make me lots of money."

"Sir, it's just a screen test," the stranger explains. "I can't guarantee she will become a movie star."

"So what? You don't know till you try."

I sigh and drag my feet across the pavement. Sweat dampens my shirt. My thighs stick together as I walk. I remember the other activities my father has prodded me to try: tennis, basketball, swimming, roller-skating, piano, and baton twirling. Regardless of whether or not I enjoy the activity, my father discontinues lessons as soon as he discovers I'm not the best at it. Once, when I wanted to take another session of roller-skating, he scoffed. "You look like an airplane with your arms sticking out," he said. "How can you win gold medal?" It didn't matter that I liked slicing through the air with my arms and legs while listening to rock 'n' roll music or that I had made a friend during the class. I was only a mediocre skater. I glance back at my sisters who stand around Lammie Pie with their mouths open and their gazes transfixed by the bright light beside the camera. Chee never asks them to try anything new. They get to do whatever they want.

"I be right back," Chee says. "Save my spot in line." He hustles over to the set.

"Your daughter has an exotic quality to her skin," the cameraman says. "Are you Chinese?"

"Hawaiian," Chee says, his standard reply to strangers. Uncle John once said Chee denies who he is to avoid prejudice and hatred. When my mother won a trip to Hawaii for the Pillsbury Bake-Off, Chee took plenty of photographs to fill his wallet. "See, here's my home," he says, showing the cameraman his Hawaiian pictures. "I live near Don Ho."

The cameraman nods. I can't tell whether or not he believes my father's story.

While the stranger talks to the cameraman, Chee bends toward me and whispers, "You do whatever he tells you, okay? Be best you can be. Make us money."

The stranger lifts his head, overhearing us. "Sir, if she makes any money, you do realize you won't have access to it. It'll be in a trust account until she turns eighteen."

"Right, right. College money." Chee lowers his voice even more. "You be movie star. Set good example for your sisters. Be rich and famous and everyone will love you. Then you can buy as many Cinderella dolls as you want, okay?"

I nod, absorbing his words, hating him for wanting me to be someone I am not.

The man introduces himself as Scott Thomas and the camera-man as Greg Fortunelli. Greg smiles and winks at me. "Whatever nationality you are, you're very pretty," he says.

"Exotic," Scott says.

"Look at her lovely eyes. Don't they look like crescent moons?" Greg says.

"And that Hollywood smile," Scott says, leading me by the shoulders to the back of the set where he asks me to stand in front of a plain gray backdrop. He stares at me for a moment longer, and I feel my heartbeat quicken and my hands sweat.

Chee stands behind Greg. He rocks back and forth on his heels and glances at Lammie Pie and my sisters as they inch forward in the ticket line.

Scott hands me a sheet of paper and instructs me to read what it says, word for word.

That is easy. It is just like memorizing my father's speeches and repeating them verbatim to relatives and strangers.

"Smile," Chee says from the distance.

I flash my teeth. Scott shakes his head. "You have a big Hollywood smile, but this is a sad scene," he explains to me. He kneels down on one knee and points to the white sheet of paper. "It's about a young woman who has lost her child. She's about to cry. The trick is to think of something that really happened to you, something that made you want to cry, and then let those feelings loose when you read the lines. It will give your performance power and believability, okay?"

I nod, thinking of the Cinderella doll we spotted in Tinker Bell's gift shop. I look at the camera, but in the periphery I see my father with his arms folded over his white T-shirt, legs astride.

I read the lines and focus on the doll I wanted, the one my father would not buy because it was too expensive. No matter how I tried to explain why I needed that particular doll, no one understood my logic. Not even my sisters. In the movie, Cinderella's dress had been a silvery-sky blue, not a baby pink. Her hair had been piled up on her head and secured with a headband and pearl earrings, not tugged carelessly into a pony tail. She wore glass slippers, not painted plastic clogs. But, no matter how sad I feel, it is not reflected in my voice. I stutter with fear and nervousness.

Scott lifts his hand. "Cut." He kneels before me and points to the words on the paper. Deep lines are etched into his face. "Relax a bit," he says. "Remember to breathe. You need to think about something else. Something more powerful. Whatever you're focused on right now isn't working. Okay? Let's try it again." He waves to Greg. "When I count to three, roll it."

Behind Scott, I glimpse Chee against the glare of the sun, his white T-shirt glowing against his brown skin. He frowns and shouts, "You can't get it right, we leave. Okay?"

"She's doing fine, sir. It was just a practice take. All right?"

I think of the other times Chee has yelled at me, demanding I be perfect, and the many times I have failed him. The memories rise up to the surface as I read, and suddenly hot tears stream down my cheeks.

Chee rushes forward. "You make her cry," he shouts.

Scott frowns and motions for Greg to stop the camera. He bats Chee away from the set. "We were filming a good scene," he explains. "But now you've interrupted the flow. We'll have to start over again."

"You make her cry," Chee repeats.

"She's supposed to cry. She's playing a woman who just lost her kid. It's called acting."

My father shakes his head. "We go now," he says, grabbing my hand.

I refuse to move. I want to tell my father what I want doesn't matter to him, and that makes me feel as if I don't matter to him. But the words jumble in my mouth and when I try to speak I start to stutter. It's easier to bunch my father's words into a ball and toss them back. "Don't you want me to be a movie star and become rich and famous?"

"I don't want to see you cry," Chee says. "It looks too real."

"It's supposed to," Scott says. "She's a good actress."

Chee changes the subject. "Tram ride almost starting. We need to find your sisters."

Scott stares directly into Chee's eyes. His voice is calm and firm. "Let her finish this," he says. "It'll only be a few more minutes. Then I can get you and your family a private tram ride, okay?"

Chee considers this for a moment, then shakes his head. "I don't want you to make her cry."

"I didn't make her cry," Scott says. A thick blue vein trembles in his neck. "It's make-believe. Pretending. Show business."

But no matter what words Scott chooses, Chee's response is the same. "No, thank you. We go now."

Chee tugs my hand, but I refuse to move. This time the tears falling from my eyes are real.

"Please, Dad, let me finish."

"I won't let this man upset you anymore," Chee says. "We go now and have a good time."

The words unknot from the base of my throat and fly out of my mouth. "You don't understand, Dad. I *want* to finish," I say, emphatically. "Why won't you let me do what I want for a change?"

"Sometimes what you want isn't good for you," he says, nullifying my emotions.

I want to tell him he's wrong, but I know he'll just say I'm as stubborn as Cynthia, and I should just surrender to his better judgment like Elizabeth. He'll compare me to my sisters just like he compares them to me, always singling out our best qualities for each other to emulate, not realizing it just pits us against one another in a constant struggle to be the best of the bunch.

Chee seems to sense my disagreement, so he continues to explain. "Sometimes you have to walk away from something that is bad for you, something that hurts," he says, indicating the tears streaming down my cheeks and dripping from my chin.

I lick my salty lips. "How can you do this to me?"

"I didn't make you cry," he says, steering me through the crowd toward my mother and sisters. They stand by the entrance gate with their purchased tickets. Their faces are expressionless under the intense sunlight.

The truth is I don't care about fame or fortune. I can walk away from a once-in-a-lifetime opportunity if it's not what I want in the moment. Sometimes my father is right, and the opportunity is a good one. Other times he is wrong, and I should just walk away. Today was a good opportunity, but I didn't have a voice in the decision. What I think or feel or say won't change the direction of my life as long as my father is around to take charge, shoving me into the roles he wants for himself, but can't have, the opportunities never given to him because he looks different than me.

I glance over my shoulder but already Scott has spotted someone else in the crowd. He bends down to talk to her, a pencil-thin girl with wispy straw-colored hair and freckles on her cheeks and arms. A pang of regret aches in my chest, but hate and confusion swirl in my head. I try to imagine how Chee will replay the scene for my sisters. Maybe he'll exaggerate my slight stutter or expound on my inability to follow directions. Either way, the story will end the same: I will have failed him and he will be blameless.

By the time we reach Lammie Pie and my sisters, the gate has opened and people are boarding the tram.

"What happened?" Elizabeth asks.

I open my mouth and hear Cynthia speak.

"She chickened out just like she did for the Miss Jr. Teen America contest."

My face burns. I don't want to remember how my father begged Joe Curly at Almaden Lincoln-Mercury to sponsor me for the pageant. I don't want to remember the swimming suit, the high heels, the dance routine Cynthia choreographed for me. I don't want to remember the fight I had with my father two weeks before the competition.

"I've changed my mind," I told Chee. My dream of walking down a runway wearing a diamond tiara with a bouquet of red roses in my arms had dissolved with the reality of how the effort to look beautiful made me feel like an object, not a human being. I went to bed feeling less like a fairy-tale princess and more like a stiff posable doll. "I don't want to do it."

"Why not?" Chee asked.

I glanced down at my hands folded in my lap. Part of me didn't know how to tell him the truth; part of me knew he wouldn't care. Chee leaned forward and rested his arms on the kitchen table. We had been practicing the art of tasteful seduction: how to smile, engage eye contact, and flirt with the flip of the hair or tilt of the chin.

"It's like prostitution," I said.

"Not prostitution."

"Yes, it is," I said, trying to explain. "I'm using my body to make money."

Chee pointed to Cynthia who stood eavesdropping by the refrigerator. "Then your sister's a prostitute. She uses her body to make money."

"That's different. She's a dancer. It takes talent to do what she does."

"And it takes talent to win beauty contest, too. All that practice," Chee said, referring to walking in three-inch heels with three books stacked on the top of my head, learning to pivot slowly and smile for the judges.

"I don't want to be famous for my body. I want to be respected for my mind."

"You get respect for your mind when you go to college with money you won from beauty contest."

I couldn't argue. I threw up my arms and asked, "Why are you making me do this?"

"I'm not making you do anything. I'm just telling you I don't have the money to send you to college. And this is a golden opportunity. Never let an opportunity pass. You never know when you'll get another one. Trust me. Most opportunities happen only once in a lifetime. Seize it." Chee banged a tight fist against the table to illustrate his point. I shuddered at the intensity of his words, the power of his conviction, the belief he had in a once-in-a-lifetime opportunity. Chee said, "You win this contest and you can go to any college you like. Princeton, Harvard, Yale, Stanford. Anywhere. You understand?"

But I didn't understand.

The next day, after Chee left for work, I phoned the directors of the Miss Jr. Teen America contest and asked for my name to be removed from the list of semi-finalists.

Cynthia's eyes narrow and she spits out, "That director only chose you because you have breasts."

"Not true!" Elizabeth shouts, linking her arm in mine. "They picked her because she can act."

"You're only saying that because she plays with you."

"Not true!"

"Yes, it is!"

"Girls! Stop fighting!" Chee shouts. "Time for tram ride. See how movies are made."

But I already know how they're made—reading other people's words over and over until a feeling, long buried, surfaces and becomes real again like finding buried treasure from Atlantis. And all the critical eyes of those watching and waiting, crossing their fingers and praying for you to get it right the first time so you can move on to the next scene and start the whole process again.

I board the tram and think, *Maybe it's good I'm not an actress. Then I don't have to worry about a script. I can be who I am, not who someone else wants me to be.* I glance at Cynthia who is sitting across from me with her arms folded over her chest. She is the closest of us girls to Chee, always seeking the American way of consumerism, using whatever talents it takes to get ahead, even if they are morally questionable. Even the shape of her round face, her pouty lower lip, and her crossed arms are like our father. Suddenly, I feel incredibly sorry for her, as if she's doomed to become what Chee is unless she can find a vehicle for escape. Like dancing. Like acting. "You're right," I tell her. "They should have chosen you."

Cynthia unfolds her arms and turns toward Elizabeth, who leans her head against my shoulder like a flower drooping in the heat. Cynthia narrows her eyes and spits, "Told you so."

Elizabeth raises her eyebrows and straightens her spine. "You're not always right. Everyone's wrong once in a while." She gazes up at me and smiles. "Except maybe Angela."

Cynthia's eyes narrow. "Angela only does what Chee tells her to do. She's like the Scarecrow in the Wizard of Oz. Only she already has a brain. She just doesn't know how to use it."

"She's smarter than you."

"Smarter? How smart is it if you can't think for yourself?" Cynthia leans back and smiles as the tram jerks forward.

Elizabeth glowers at her, then looks questioningly at me. "Is it true?"

"Who makes up the best stories? Cynthia or me?"

"You do."

"And they don't come out of a book, do they?"

"No, they come out of your head."

"Then I guess that answers your question." I glare at Cynthia although I'm still talking to Elizabeth. "I *can* think for myself."

Cynthia shakes her head. "Don't look at me like that."

"Why not?" I challenge.

"Because it's rude."

"And what you said about me isn't?"

"Truth hurts," she says, falling back on the maxim.

By the end of the afternoon, we have seen everything there is to see, from animal actors to a stunt show. The sun is setting fast, streaking violet and orange across an otherwise blue sky. The subtle breeze that has followed us all afternoon suddenly picks up speed, blowing our curls across our eyes and prickling our skin with goose bumps. Chee rubs his arms and says, "Let's get an early dinner and go home."

We pile into the van and drive north. Lammie Pie glances up from her cross-stitch and asks, "Can we stop at a real restaurant? I don't want hot dogs or hamburgers."

"Whatever you want, sweetheart," he says. There is a lilt in his voice, a rare softness that penetrates the usual tension. I wonder what has changed.

We stop at Bob's Big Boy. Chee orders a steak and baked potatoes. Cynthia, Elizabeth, and I order fish and chips. Lammie Pie requests a house salad with Italian dressing on the side.

While we wait for our orders to be delivered, Chee fumbles with the sugar packets on the table. "Not everything is good for you," he begins. "Like the screen test. Waste of time. You never make it as an actress. Just look on TV. No Chinese men or women. They're all white. Maybe one or two are black. That's it."

"But I'm half white," I say, challenging him.

"No one believes you when they look at your slanted eyes," Chee says.

"Just like no one believes you when you say you're Hawaiian."

Chee stops fidgeting with the sugar packets and stares at me dumbfounded. It is the first time I have dared to confront him about anything.

I take advantage of the silence to push my argument further. "Cynthia should give up dancing then. She looks the most Chinese out of all of us," I say, referring to me and my sisters. "There are no Chinese ballerinas."

Cynthia's eyes widen. She opens her mouth to speak, but Lammie Pie cuts her off.

"Angela, don't bring your sister into this." Turning to our father, she adds, "Dave, leave your daughter alone. I want to eat in peace."

The waitress hovers beside our table, her arms laden with plates. She smiles awkwardly at our conversation. "Should I come back?"

"No, no, no," Chee smiles. "Here, let me help you."

The fish are hot and greasy and the fries are salty and crisp. My sisters and I wipe our hands on the cloth napkins and gulp our glasses of milk.

"Slow down," Chee says. "The food isn't going to run away."

Cynthia giggles and makes her fingers into a pair of legs skirting across the tablecloth. We burst into laughter.

When we are finished eating, Chee examines our plates. "You forgot best part of meal," he says, picking up a slice of orange.

"You're not supposed to eat that," Lammie Pie says.

"Why not?" Chee asks, chewing on the pulp against the rind.

"It's garnish."

"When we were kids, we did not eat dessert," Chee explains. "We were too poor. If we were lucky, we might have an orange. Each one of us would get a slice after our bowl of rice and vegetables."

"We were poor, too," Lammie Pie says, "but we always had dessert. Mom baked cookies with M&M's instead of chocolate chips, because they were cheaper. But my favorite dessert was Jell-O. My dad would never eat it because it wiggled. He thought it was alive. So, he'd give his bowl to me."

"Two desserts?" Elizabeth asks.

Lammie Pie nods. "How do you think I got so fat?"

"You're not fat," Elizabeth says. "You're chubby like me."

Lammie Pie smiles between bites of a tomato. "You're sweet," she says.

After dinner, we walk back to the van for the long ride home. Already the sky is black and cloudless. The air is dry and chill. I tug my sweater over my breasts and shiver. Lammie Pie takes the driver's seat. Elizabeth lies down across the bench seat and draws a blanket over her body. Cynthia places the headphones over her ears. Chee tilts his chair back until his head is practically in my lap. Within minutes, he is snoring. When the snores settle into a predictable pattern, Lammie Pie searches for a good radio station. Saxophone riffs waft through the van. I stare out the window at the black sky and the passing cars. The drone of the freeway and the jazzy melody hypnotize me. My eyes grow heavy. I glance over at Cynthia. Her head bobs against her chest. I fight to stay awake, to think up a new story for my sisters to tell them tomorrow when we are home, but before I can come up with a plot, I fall asleep.

7: HOME IMPROVEMENTS

When we return to San Jose, Chee is disgusted by the appearance of the front lawn. Its deep-green shaggy overgrowth spills outside the perfect square perimeter Chee has worked so hard to maintain. Grandpa was supposed to water the lawn every other day and pick up the newspaper and the mail. Chee stands outside the house with his arms crossed over his chest, hands tucked in his armpits, frowning. "He didn't mow it," Chee complains.

"You didn't ask him to," Lammie Pie explains. "I'm sure he would have, if you'd asked him."

Chee stoops to remove a weed from the sidewalk. He flicks the tangled roots into the garbage can and points to my sisters and me. "Go to the shed. Get the clippers. I mow, you trim," he says.

My sisters and I change into our rags, soiled shirts and polyester pants with patches over the knees. It is the same outfit we wear whenever we visit his boss at the grocery store. The last time we wore these clothes Chee's boss gave him overtime and a raise. "He thinks we're poor," Chee said, smiling over the bigger paycheck. "Let him. We can always use extra money."

Cynthia, Elizabeth, and I kneel at different corners of the lawn and begin trimming. Within a few minutes, my eyes blur and my nose runs. I wipe the snot with the back of my hand and continue clipping the blades of grass away from the edge of the sidewalk. I sneeze. Snot dribbles over my chin and down my shirt.

"Get a tissue," Chee says.

I stand up and hurry into the garage. Lammie Pie is sorting clothes into the washing machine. She stops me.

"What's wrong?" she asks.

"My allergies," I sniff. "Dad wants me to get a tissue."

"You shouldn't be mowing the lawn. Why can't he do it himself?"

I duck into the kitchen to retrieve a box of tissue. When I return, Lammie Pie has gathered the girls under her arms and is yelling at Chee.

"They can't do this," she says. "They'll be sick for days. Mow and trim the lawn yourself. Or pay a neighbor to."

Chee scrunches up his lips.

Lammie Pie ushers us into the house. "Go change and shower," she suggests."I'll make you some hot lemon water to drink."

After an hour of mowing and trimming the lawn by himself, Chee slaps open the kitchen door and announces, "No more lawn. Too much work without the kids to help. We'll pour concrete."

"Just concrete?" Lammie Pie asks. "How about bricks? It's prettier."

"Cost too much," Chee says.

"But concrete is ugly," Lammie Pie says.

"We'll get estimates."

The following week, the contractor arrives. After cementing the front yard, Chee decides to replace the dark carpet in the living room and paint the walls white. "More light," he says.

The transformation inspires Chee. "We'll paint the whole house outside."

"I like lemon yellow," Lammie Pie says. "It's soft and inviting."

"I like red for happiness," Chee says.

After several trips to Kelly-Moore Paints, our simple blue-and-yellow house now glows like a stoplight. Neighbors phone the police, wondering what they can do. The police drive-by, but do not stop to speak with us, for there is no homeowner's association, no covenants and restrictions. We are free to paint our house any color we choose.

The notoriety of our home spreads beyond the neighborhood. Strangers cruise by and idle beside the curb. A reporter from the

Mercury News rings the doorbell and asks if he can come inside and take pictures of Buddha. Chee points to the white rock garden beside the now flaming-red porch. A three-foot white bisque statue of Buddha with red rhinestone jewels sits cross-legged with his hands open, palms up.

"My wife made that," he says, proudly. "She's very talented. Cook, sew, paint, sculpt. You wrote an article about her winning the Pillsbury Bake-Off contest in 1971."

"That must have been one of my colleagues, sir," the reporter says, taking notes. "I've only worked at the paper the last two years." He stops to scratch his chin with the blunt end of the pen. "When are services?"

"Services?"

"Worship."

"We worship God, not Buddha," Chee explains. "We're Catholic."

The reporter wrinkles his brow. "Isn't this a Buddhist temple?"

"No, this is our home."

"Then why'd you paint your house red and yellow?"

"For good luck," Chee says, proudly. He points to the lions flanking either side of the front door. They have been painted fire-engine red with fluorescent yellow eyes. "My wife made these, too. If you want to interview her for paper, you go to her work, okay? She's dressed nice today. Three-piece suit I bought for her at Macy's. She's lost twenty-five pounds. And she has a new perm. She'll look good in photo. Is this for front page?"

The reporter shakes his head and mumbles, "I'm sorry, sir. This has been a huge mistake. There will be no story. I thought this was a Buddhist temple, not your private residence."

Chee looks disappointed. He closes the red front door with the yellow bubble-glass window and sighs. "We were almost famous."

Cynthia giggles.

"What's so funny?" Chee asks.

"You are," she says, laughing, "and the reporter, and the police, and the people who drive by really slow."

"Why's that funny?"

"Because you didn't think before you painted the house. You just painted it any color you chose. Because the reporter thought the house was a temple. Because the police are too scared to come knock on our front door. They probably think we're crazy. And the people who drive by think we're a freak show."

"So, what're you saying?"

Cynthia closes her mouth and suddenly looks serious. "You should think things through, first. And not be afraid to change your mind if you're wrong."

"What's wrong with painting a house red and yellow? It's good luck."

"We aren't in China," Cynthia says. "We're in America. Good luck doesn't exist here."

"Why you say that? I won $25,000, didn't I?"

"You've lost more than that before."

"How do you know? You always think you know everything. If that were true, then how come you don't come home with better grades?"

Cynthia rolls her eyes. "You're impossible. I'm not talking book-smarts. I'm talking common sense."

Chee storms down the hall to his bedroom. "I have to get ready for work," he says. "I have to make extra money to pay for your remedial classes because you're too smart to study."

Cynthia wanders into the living room and turns on the TV. "How stupid," she says, when Tom and Jerry race across the screen, playing cat and mouse. "They're nothing but idiots."

"Who is?" Elizabeth asks, sitting cross-legged next to her.

Cynthia throws up her arms. "Dad, the reporter, everyone!"

8: FRIENDS

A week later, I ride my green Schwinn three-speed bike around the neighborhood after dinner.

Since Chee is at work, Lammie Pie agrees to let me go by myself. "Just don't be gone too long," she says, studying the sky. "I want you home before the sun sets."

The wind blows through my frizzy permed hair. The air smells of smoke from barbecues and the sweet perfume of roses from the neighbor's yard. I ride past Laura's house and glance through the large picture window in the living room, but it looks like no one is home. I cringe, remembering how Laura and I used to be best friends all through elementary school until fifth grade when a Korean immigrant, Christine, moved into the house around the block. When Christine was a chapter behind in Amidon, she made me promise to wait for her to catch up. "That way we can start studying together and moving up together and finish the series together. We'll even share the prize for finishing first. What fun is eating an ice cream sundae all alone?" Although I felt uncomfortable about the offer, I agreed to wait. After the second week, I asked Christine when she thought she would be done with the current chapter so we could start studying together. That's when I discovered she had not only caught up to me, but had surpassed me by two chapters. To make things worse, she had solicited Laura's friendship, and the two of them finished the series first, sharing the ice cream sundae without me. When I told Chee what happened, he said, "That's why you have sisters, so you have someone to play with, someone who understands you, someone who will always be faithful. You don't need friends. See what they do? They only betray you."

Now whenever I go by Laura's house, I feel a pang of sorrow over the years of friendship that dissolved almost instantly with Christine's cunning. I know I'm still bitter over the whole ordeal, because last year when Laura started crying at school during recess about her parents getting a divorce, I didn't offer to console her or listen to her or even pretend to understand. I just asked, "Where's Christine? I thought she was your best friend."

We haven't spoken to each other since, and although I am lonely for someone my age to spend time with, I have no plans on starting now.

The next house I pass belongs to Heather, who is closer to Cynthia's age. She has freckled skin and long arms. She and her half sister compete in Highland Scottish dances with their mother who remarried a Japanese man when her Scottish husband passed away. I once tried confiding in Heather about my situation at home, being the oldest, shouldering so much responsibility, trying hard to live up to the high expectations my Chinese-American father places on me thinking she might understand, since her stepfather is Japanese and seems to be no different than my father. But she only shrugged. "I like everything my parents ask me to do," she said. "I want to compete and be the best I can be." She spread her arms wide and smiled. "I want my whole room full of trophies for dancing."

I cross the street and ride into the court past Greg's house. In kindergarten, Greg and I used to be boyfriend and girlfriend until Chee banned him from our home, saying he only came over to eat bananas and ride our Big Wheels bike and crash it into the house. "I have to buy more food whenever he comes over and fix paint on the house," Chee explained to Greg's parents over the phone when they called to ask if Greg could come over for a visit when I was almost six. We still smile whenever we pass each other at school, but we don't talk. It's like Greg is more afraid of me than he is of my father.

At the center of the court, a moving van is parked in the driveway.

A young woman with big brown hair and a red smile waves to me. "Hey, slow down," she says. "I want to talk to you."

I brake and straddle my bike, pushing my curls off my sweaty forehead. Up close, I realize the young woman is a girl like me. Breathing hard, I wait a moment before introducing myself.

The girl takes my hand. Her nails are painted the same red as her lips. "I'm Antoinette," she says, winking. "How old are you?"

"I'm going to be twelve in August. And you?"

"I'm already twelve. I'll be thirteen in December." She squints. "You go to Morrill or Sierramont Middle School?"

"Sierramont," I tell her. "And you?"

She snickers, as if laughing at a secret joke. "I don't go to either."

"No school?"

"I never said that. You're assuming. Assuming is the quickest way to get into trouble. It's like saying you know something that you don't. And that can make people upset because they think you don't understand them when the real problem is you just aren't paying attention or asking the right questions or waiting long enough to actually hear the response." Antoinette's brown eyes twinkle and her mouth twists into a half smile, so I know she's not upset with me for assuming things about her. Although she said she was twelve, she looks a lot older. Maybe sixteen or seventeen. She wears a white Guess T-shirt and dark-blue Jordache jeans, the same brands of clothing Cynthia pines for. On her, the clothes look just as good as they do on the girls in the advertisements. *Maybe she's a model*, I think. But I'm too afraid to ask.

Antoinette tilts her head and studies me. "Want to come inside?"

I glance around, but there is no one behind me telling me what to do. My hands grip the handlebars. I have to decide on my own.

"I go to private school." Antoinette lifts her eyebrows and traces an invisible line with one foot. She steps closer to me and wiggles her finger, baiting me with a promise. "I'll tell you all about it once we're inside."

My hands pulse with the same rhythm as my heart. I want to talk with Antoinette. She doesn't know me. She doesn't know my father. I can have another chance at making a friend. Remembering Lammie

Pie's warning, I glance at the orange sky streaked with purple. *If I stay for five minutes, I'll have plenty of time to get home.*

I park my bike against the moving van and slip into Antoinette's stuffy house. In the kitchen, we pass her parents who are taking a break from unpacking. They sit at a small round table and share a cup of coffee and a package of cigarettes. "Who's your friend?" her mother asks.

"This is Angela," Antoinette says. "She goes to Sierramont Middle School."

Her mother leans back in the chair and coughs. She isn't as pretty as Antoinette. She pulls her curls into a severe bun and wears no makeup. Although she sports the same T-shirt and jeans, she doesn't appear glamorous. Her body is bone-hard and leathery, as if she has weathered more than her fair share of life's storms. Her husband sits silently beside her, curling his burly back over his coffee cup, his eyes shielded with a baseball cap.

"You girls going to play dolls?" Antoinette's mother asks.

"Sure," Antoinette says. Taking me by the arm, she leads me down the hall into her room and closes the door. Sitting cross-legged on the floor, she searches through one of the many boxes stacked in towers over the carpet and tugs a few Barbies out and passes one to me.

I stare at the unkempt doll with her flyaway hair and crumpled clothes and ask, "What's her name?"

Antoinette frowns. "What do you mean? She's Barbie. They're all Barbie."

"My dolls all have names. They all have histories. They all have families."

Antoinette tilts her head back and laughs. "Why would you go through the trouble of naming them and creating stories about them? They're only dolls."

I flush with embarrassment.

"Tell me about school," I say.

Antoinette unfolds her legs and stretches out on the carpet between two stacks of boxes. She bites her lower lip and rolls her eyes up toward the ceiling. "I got suspended too many times, so they kicked me out of my last school. Now I have to go private until I can prove to my parents and the administrators that I've got my act together." She shakes her head and curls her legs under her hips and leans close to me. "It doesn't make sense. They're just a bunch of hypocrites."

"What doesn't make sense? Who's a hypocrite?"

"I got busted for smoking. My parents smoke. If it's so bad for you, why don't they quit?"

I nod, understanding her logic. When Elizabeth stole a pack of gum and Chee demanded she return it to the store manager, Elizabeth said the same thing, "If it's wrong to steal, why do you do it?"

Antoinette sighs. "I thought once we moved to another part of the city, my parents would let me go to either Morrill or Sierramont, but they don't trust me yet. My older sister ran away when she was sixteen and came back with a baby. My mother says thirty-eight is too young to be a grandmother. But she is. And she swears she doesn't want that to happen to me. But I tell her not to worry. I'm not interested in boys, only smoking. And isn't smoking for you better than having sex?"

She stares at me like I should know. But I don't. I have never smoked and I have never had sex.

She examines the way I hold the Barbie doll, the way I caress her hair, the way I straighten her clothes. "You must have younger sisters," she says.

"Two of them."

"Are they just like you? Do they name their dolls and make up stories about them?"

I nod.

Antoinette chuckles until she coughs. "You're strange. But I like you."

I glance out the window. The sky is almost dark. I hand back the doll and stand up. "I have to go."

"Why? You just got here."

"I have to be home. I promised."

"Why don't you call and tell your parents you're going to be late?

That's what my mother asks of me. She says everything is okay as long as she knows where I am and what time I expect to be back."

I don't want to be rude, but I don't have time to explain. Opening the door, I stomp down the hall and say good-bye over my shoulder. Outside, the air is frighteningly cool. A strip of orange remains in the otherwise purple sky. I straddle my bike and start to pedal. Antoinette screams behind me. "I like you. Will you come back again?"

I glance over my shoulder and shout, "I'll try. No promises."

When I get home, Lammie Pie places her hands on her hips and asks what took me so long. When I hesitate, she says, "Next time, we're all going with you. I'll ride in the front. Cynthia and Elizabeth will ride in the middle. And you'll ride in the back. I'll stop every couple of minutes to make sure you're still behind us, okay?"

I swallow hard and sigh. *Why argue?* I think. *She'll only get upset and tell Chee, and then none of us will get to bike anywhere without him.*

The next couple of weeks, we ride our bikes for a half hour after dinner. But whenever we pass Antoinette's house, she is not outside. I do not ask to stop so I can go up to her door and see if she's home. Although we don't seem to have a lot in common, something about her intrigues me. Maybe it is her ease and sophistication. Maybe it is her sense of righteousness over her hypocritical parents. Whatever it is, I like it so much I want it for me.

Finally, when I think I will never see her again, she appears walking across the street just outside our kitchen window. Chee is home, eating dinner with us, and he notices her the same moment as I do.

"Who's that girl?" he asks.

"Antoinette," I say, before thinking of the consequences. "She moved into the court a couple of weeks ago. She's my age."

Chee stares at her, puckering his lips, digesting what I said. "She looks older."

"*I* look older."

"No, I don't mean that."

"What do you mean?" I spear a piece of chicken Chee cooked and shove it into my mouth, wondering how he will answer.

He continues to stare at Antoinette through the window, as

if he is memorizing her features. Finally, he says, "She looks . . . experienced."

Cynthia glances out the window and spies Antoinette just before she disappears from our view. "Slut," she says.

Elizabeth gasps. "You said a bad word."

Chee nods. "You're both right." He glances at Lammie Pie. "Have you met her parents?"

Lammie Pie shakes her head. When she turns her gaze to me, I duck my head toward my plate and focus on the rice, chicken, and peas.

"You know her?" Chee asks me.

"I saw her once, that's all. She said hi and introduced herself. That's all."

Chee sighs. "Stay away from her. She's nothing but trouble."

Although I want to appeal to Lammie Pie for support, even she is forbidden to have friendships. When Chee is at work, she talks with Joanne on the phone, a woman she works with, a woman she would otherwise call a friend, if Chee didn't have a problem with that word. Sometimes she goes out for drinks with Joanne after dinner on Tuesday and Thursday nights, Chee's days off. She'd tell him she was doing something else, and he believed her until one night, after drinking too much, she stumbled into the kitchen singing. He pulled her close, smelled her breath, and pushed her away. That was the last time she went out with Joanne.

"You like Uncle Jong," Chee says to my mother, "a disgrace to the family."

Lammie Pie giggles and waves. "Bye, bye, Miss American Pie," she sings.

My sisters and I join with her, "Drove my Chevy to the levy but the levy was dry. And them good ol' boys were drinkin' whiskey and rye, singing this'll be the day that I die!" We link our arms together and sway back and forth in a silly shuffle. Lammie Pie is one of us, a child without cares, laughing at our strict and sullen father.

"You come home right after work," Chee demands. "Or else—"

"Or else?" Lammie Pie asks.

"Or else you quit your job."

The smile vanishes from her face. "You can't make me quit. What about Cynthia's dance lessons?"

"You stay home and sew costumes for tuition."

Lammie Pie draws in a quick breath. My sisters and I gather around her, squeezing her hands, trying to infuse strength against Chee's threat.

But, in the end, she exhales. Her shoulders slope with silent defeat. We scuttle to our rooms, afraid of our father's wrath.

For a while, Lammie Pie resists the urge to visit with Joanne. Several times a week, she picks up the phone, dials, and hangs up. By the end of the second week, she shakes with panic while we are cleaning the kitchen after lunch.

"I have to get out," she says. "I can't stand it anymore."

"Stand what?" Elizabeth asks. She removes plates from the dishwasher and hands them to me. I stack them in the cupboards. Cynthia wipes the table and sweeps the floor. It is our routine after every meal. Lammie Pie lifts the curtain ruffle and glances into the side yard where Chee stomps on aluminum cans and tosses them into a huge plastic bag to exchange for money at the downtown recycling center. The creases on the sides of her mouth twitch.

"At least you still get to work," Cynthia says.

"It's not the same," Lammie Pie says, wistfully. She releases the curtain and it flutters against the glass. She turns and smiles at us. "Someday when you have children, you'll understand how difficult it is to lead your own life."

"I'm not having kids," Cynthia says. "Too much responsibility."

"My husband will let me do whatever I want," I tell her. "Or I'll leave him."

She smiles, amused.

"Maybe you and Daddy should go out together," Elizabeth suggests. "Like a date."

"I don't know if he'd take me."

"Sure, he would. Angela will babysit us, won't you?" Elizabeth looks imploringly at me.

I nod, not really wanting to babysit, but not really wanting to see my mother so sad.

Lammie Pie decides to take Elizabeth's advice. The following Thursday night Chee picks her up from work and takes her to dinner and a movie. When I come home from school, there is a note written on the back of a paper grocery bag in thick black permanent ink. "Angela: Preheat oven to 375° and cook for 45 minutes. Love, Daddy." In the refrigerator, a plastic bag of Shake 'N Bake chicken rests on a metal baking sheet. At four fifteen, I turn on the oven. My sisters lie on their stomachs on the pink carpet watching TV in the living room, their feet twirling around in tiny circles from their bent knees, their chins cupped in their palms, elbows propped against the carpet. I want to join them, but I can't. I still have to chop up broccoli and carrots and steam some rice. From the cabinet beside the sink, I remove a pot and dip my finger into it as I fill it with water from the sink. I wait until the water level reaches the knuckle of my finger before I turn the water off and put the pot on the stove and spoon in a cup of rice. Covering the pot, I turn the burners down and start chopping vegetables on a butcher block on the tile counter by the sink. From the living room, I hear the theme music of my favorite cartoon, Star Blazers, and I pause to peek at the oven door, which reflects the TV screen perfectly.

When Lammie Pie started working, I thought maybe Chee might hire a sitter, someone older and wiser who was paid money to watch us play. But he didn't. The more money he had, the more vigilant he was with it, as if it might disappear. "Why waste money on a sitter when I could spend it on you?" Chee once said. But the money never was spent on us. Everything we had was stolen or paid for by money Lammie Pie earned. Nothing came from the money saved, not counting the vacation to Lake Tahoe, which never really seemed like a vacation, just another location to babysit my sisters. Again.

Sometimes I hate being the oldest, being the one Chee expects to be responsible and mature, always ready to chip in or supervise. Sometimes I wish I was Cynthia, Lammie Pie's beloved, or Elizabeth, the baby who gets away with everything. Sometimes I wish I had an older brother to shoulder the responsibility. But I'm not Cynthia or Elizabeth, and I don't have an older sibling. So, here I am, on a Thursday evening, cooking dinner for my sisters while my parents are off on a date.

When dinner is ready, my sisters sit at the table and pick at their food, staring at each other like in an old Western showdown, each one waiting for the other to take the first bite. "Eat," I tell them. But the chicken is too crispy and the vegetables are a watery mush. After begging and cajoling, I finally give up in bitterness and frustration.

A half hour later, the garage door rattles up and the kitchen door opens. Chee and Lammie Pie titter over some private joke. I slump at the table with my sisters who have not taken one bite of food.

"Still eating?" Chee asks, glancing at his watch.

"Just finished," I say, standing up and avoiding his gaze.

Lammie Pie sets her purse down on the counter and helps me put the leftovers away. Her hands are perfumed, soft, and white with long fingers. Those talented fingers can mend a shirt or wipe a tear away. I glance at my own hands, which could be a mirror of my mother's hands, and smile at the talent they possess to draw almost anything.

"Did you have fun?" I ask, hoping my small sacrifice was worth the effort to make my mother happy.

"Yes, I did," she says, with her soft voice. Her blue gaze caresses me, and for a moment, I feel closer to her than I ever have. Sharing the burden of cooking dinner has brought me a tiny bit of understanding about the world she inhabits, a world where gratitude for nourishment is taken for granted. Only she doesn't take me for granted. She touches my shoulder and says, "Thank you for watching your sisters."

I smile shyly at her, accepting her gratitude, silently wishing there was more I could do to keep that lovely smile on her face.

9: LAMMIE PIE'S COMPANY PICNIC

In July, Lammie Pie asks Chee if she can go to her company's picnic. "Everyone will be there," she says. "It's being held at Mr. Buckley's house. He has a huge swimming pool and Jacuzzi. There'll be games and movies and sunbathing and lots of food. Everyone is bringing a dish. I thought I might make something simple this time—no Chinese bowties or lemon chicken. Maybe a fruit salad with a tropical twist."

We are gathered in the living room. Cynthia and Elizabeth are watching TV. Chee and I are folding laundry. Lammie Pie stands with her back to the flickering screen. She has lost so much weight she looks like the silhouette of a movie star with the bright lights and shadows flickering over her long, soft waves of hair and classic hour-glass figure.

Chee lifts a towel from the basket and folds it neatly into a square and adds it to the towering stack on the sofa. "Why you want to go?" he asks, without looking at her. "You see them every day at work."

"It's a party," Lammie Pie says. "That's different than work. I never get to talk to them as people."

"What about Wednesday night bowling?"

"That's different. It's about competition. We're too busy thinking about winning to talk about anything else."

Chee purses his lips.

"What about the kids?" Chee asks, groping for a ready excuse.

"It's on a Saturday afternoon. You can watch them till you leave for work."

"No," Chee says. "I have other things to do on Saturday. Somebody needs to watch the kids. Remember last time I washed the car and Cynthia cut Elizabeth with a scissors? We had to go to emergency because you weren't home. Angela had to cook dinner from scratch. I came home to a complete mess." Chee shakes his head. "Maybe next year you go."

There is a moment of tense silence before Lammie Pie announces, "I'm going this year, even if I have to take the children with me."

"Is anybody else bringing kids?" Chee asks.

Lammie Pie shrugs. "It doesn't matter. I'm going." She saunters out of the living room and disappears down the hallway. Her bedroom door clicks shut.

Chee turns to me and says, "Your mom doesn't understand there are some things kids shouldn't see. You going to watch your sisters if your mom takes you to the party?" It is a half question, half statement, tinged with meaning beyond my comprehension. I hold my breath and clench the towel in my hands. I don't know what to say so I continue to stare at him blankly.

I think about Lammie Pie's protests when Chee showed me issues of *Playboy* to illustrate the phenomenon of female adolescence when I started getting breasts last year. "She doesn't need to see that, Dave," Lammie Pie said, snatching away the magazine.

"I'm educating her," Chee explained. "She needs to know why she needs to do push-ups. To get big, firm breasts to get a good husband."

"All she'll get with big breasts are offers to get laid!"

"Aiyaah! She's smarter than that. She won't get laid."

Lammie Pie tore up the magazine. The glossy bits of breasts and thighs fluttered over the linoleum floor in the kitchen. "What if your other daughters came in from playing outside and saw this?" she demanded. "What would you tell them?"

"That I'm educating their sister. That there are things she needs to know."

Now, with the prospect of socially mingling with real-life adults, Chee seems compelled to shield me, protect me, insulate me from things I should not know.

I decide to silently agree, while I wonder what has changed in my mother to make her so bold as to defy my father's request whatever the cost.

Two weeks later, Lammie Pie rushes into the kitchen where Chee is fixing sandwiches for lunch. "Don't waste your time, Dave. They're coming with me."

"They need to eat first."

"They'll eat at the party. C'mon," she says, ushering us into the kitchen. She is wearing a clinging turquoise-blue tank top, which highlights the startling blue of her eyes, and a new pair of shorts, showcasing the new slimness of her thighs. Her skin is milky, much paler than my golden skin that has deepened into a soft brown over the summer. She wears a pair of sandals and folds a beach towel in the crook of her arm. "Just in case anyone wants to swim," she says.

I grab the plastic container of fruit salad from the refrigerator. Cynthia struts into the kitchen in her red tube top sprinkled with tiny flowers and denim jeans Lammie Pie bought on clearance at Mervyn's. In her Jordache handbag, she carries her swimsuit, towel, and beauty supplies. A pair of sunglasses perches on the top of her head. Elizabeth is wearing her swimsuit with one of Lammie Pie's T-shirts over it.

Chee pulls me aside and says, "You keep an eye on your mom and your sisters, okay? Tell me everything that happens."

We pack into the Club Wagon van. Since Chee is not coming with us, I sit in the front seat next to Lammie Pie. I feel powerful and omniscient. I wonder if Chee will let me drive the van when I get my license in a few years.

Lammie Pie tunes the radio to KARA in Santa Clara. Cynthia shouts, "Let's listen to something else."

"Like what?"

"Modern rock," she says, moving to the front of the van and turning the knob.

A blast of electric guitars and steel drums rattle through the van as a man's warbling voice zigzags between us.

Lammie Pie turns the volume down a notch and continues driving.

"I hope you'll find something to do," Lammie Pie says to me, the only one who hasn't brought a swimsuit.

"I'm supposed to watch my sisters," I say.

"You don't have to do that."

"What else am I supposed to do?"

"Have fun." Lammie Pie smiles and winks at me. "You spend all your time during the school year locked up in your room. You should go outside and have fun. Unlike what your father thinks, there's more to life than education."

I don't bother to confess I prefer being alone in my room, that I am not always studying, that sometimes I draw pictures of fairy-tale women in beautiful turn-of-the century gowns or compose poems and love letters to boys who will never speak to me, other than to ask, "May I copy from your test?"

We turn down a street lined with two-story houses flanked with tiny trees. Lammie Pie parks the van against the curb. She carries the bowl of fruit salad. Cynthia and Elizabeth hold my hands as we walk up the cement path to the double doors. A bald man who looks like a cross between Mr. Clean and a cowboy with a beer belly pulls back the door. "Margaret, glad you could come," he says, holding a plastic cup of beer in one hand and pulling her close with the other hand to kiss her cheek. She blushes against his checkered shirt. "These must be your kids," he says, glancing down at us with a twinkle in his bleary eyes. "I'm Mr. Buckley, your mom's boss." He takes turns shaking our hands. "What's wrong?" he asks Elizabeth, who's holding her tummy. "Are you hungry?" She shakes her head and whispers, "I have to go potty."

He waves to a thin woman wearing a plain white sundress. "Sally, dear, why don't you show this young lady to the bathroom?" The thin woman gives a little nod and guides Elizabeth out of the room.

"Sally's my sister. She's visiting from Oklahoma." Mr. Buckley nudges us toward the kitchen. "There's plenty of food. I'll help you make a plate, okay?"

In the kitchen, bowls of potato salad, macaroni salad, three-bean salad, rice, burritos, lasagna, and Lammie Pie's fruit salad cover the tile counters. Mr. Buckley responds to Cynthia's requests by only putting what she wants in the amount she wants on her plate. When he hands it to her, Lammie Pie walks up and asks, "Can you make me one, too?"

"Same things?" he asks.

"No, I want more three-bean salad and less potato salad," she says. "And you can skip the rice."

"What about you?" he asks me.

"Oh, I can help myself," I say.

"Why not let me help you? I already helped your mom and your sister."

"Oh, okay," I shrug, not wanting to insult him. He seems to be a kind man and I suddenly see why Lammie Pie likes him. It's not because he looks like the Malibu Ken doll or any of the rich men on the evening soap opera, *Dallas*. It's because he genuinely cares.

Elizabeth returns from the bathroom and accepts a plate of food from Mr. Buckley. My sisters and I sit on the couch in the family room in front of the TV, which no one has bothered to turn on. Behind us, through the sliding glass door, people splash in the pool. Elizabeth mumbles something about how she can't swim after eating, so she tucks her plate beneath the lamp on the side table and goes outside to the pool. Cynthia nudges me to follow her and we find two lounge chairs beside a table with an umbrella and sit with our plates to eat.

A little Chihuahua dog scuttles over to us and sniffs our feet. He wanders around the pool party and finds a plastic cup of beer someone left in the grass. "Look, Ang," Cynthia says, nudging me. "He's drinking it!"

Sure enough, the dog laps the amber liquid with zeal. He doesn't move away for a long time.

"Hey, Margaret, are you going to swim?" someone asks from the pool.

Lammie Pie stands under an arbor tree with Mr. Buckley. She says, "I don't think so, Joanne. I'd have to change into my swimsuit."

Mr. Buckley pinches her side. "Ah, c'mon, Margaret. Give us a show."

Lammie Pie blushes again.

Joanne crosses her arms and leans them on the ledge of the pool. She doesn't look as dangerous as Chee has made her out to be. Her dark hair sticks out like steel wool and her eyes glitter with mischief against the backdrop of leathery skin. She looks about ten years older than Lammie Pie although Lammie Pie has said she's three years younger. "We want to know how you did it, losing thirty pounds in thirty days," Joanne says, coming out of the pool. Joanne's swagger suggests a world of knowledge. With one hand, she gulps a glass of margarita and pours herself another. "C'mon. I'll help you undress." She reaches for Lammie Pie's hand and leads her into the house.

More and more adults wander into and out of the house carrying drinks. The more they drink, the louder they get. My shoulders start to cramp. This isn't an organized party hosted by the Lam family where everyone eats quietly and leaves. People throw others into the pool. They chew macaroni salad with their mouths open. They shout and curse. I wince, wondering what my father would say if he knew. Cynthia sits with her sunglasses over her eyes, as relaxed as if she naturally belonged to this crowd. I try to practice her stance by crossing my leg over my knee, but I feel clumsy and awkward. I uncross my legs and stand up to stretch the crick in my neck before sitting down again. I don't know how to behave in this environment.

The Chihuahua has finished lapping up the beer in the plastic cup, tipping it over to get to the rest and spilling it in the grass. He hobbles in a crooked line around the maze of feet looking for another cup to drink. Cynthia slaps the table and laughs. "He's drunk! The dog's drunk!"

The sliding glass door opens and Lammie Pie steps out in her flip-flops wearing a floral one-piece swimsuit. People hoot and holler and clap. Lammie Pie struts and turns like a runway model and smiles shyly for the crowd. "Wow!" Mr. Buckley says, spilling his beer. When she catches his comment, she blushes again.

"You look absolutely fabulous," Mr. Buckley says. "Better than Marilyn Monroe."

Lammie Pie dips her head; her eyelashes slightly flutter. Cynthia nudges me. "Look! Mom's flirting! She likes Mr. Buckley."

I hold my breath and hiss, "Shut up. She's just shy, that's all."

Cynthia tips her head back and laughs. "You're so naive, it's funny."

Lammie Pie slips away from the crowd of people and wades into the pool. Elizabeth wraps her arms around Lammie Pie's neck and snuggles against her. "You should have come in earlier," Elizabeth says. "I'm hungry." Elizabeth swims away from Lammie Pie and walks up the steps, shaking water from her body. She wraps herself up in a towel and bolts inside to retrieve her food.

"Why don't you go change into the extra clothes I brought for you," Cynthia says. "We'll watch your food."

Elizabeth's eyes widen. "You brought clothes for me?"

Cynthia nods. "Don't go getting all mushy on me. It's nothing fashionable. Just a T-shirt and shorts with an elastic waistband. Last year's style."

Elizabeth rustles through the bag at Cynthia's feet and finds the clothes. She hustles into the house to change.

While she is gone, Cynthia shoos flies away from Elizabeth's plate before deciding to pin a napkin over the food with cans of soda left on the table. The Chihuahua jumps on her leg, sniffing and pawing, eyeing the soda cans. Cynthia laughs and jerks her leg, knocking the dog's balance. He stumbles back and whimpers.

"You stupid dog, it's not beer," Cynthia says. "You should go inside and sober up. If you drink anymore, you might have a hangover."

The Chihuahua scampers away, sniffing and pawing at other guests, searching for more beer.

"Whose dog is it anyway?" I ask.

Cynthia shrugs, her gaze transfixed by the commotion inside. "Oh, my god," she says, "look at this."

I turn toward her gaze and notice Mr. Buckley, with his hands full of two cups of beer, smash his face against the sliding glass door. The bump rattles the glass like a clap of thunder and everyone in the pool glances up to see what happened. Cynthia suppresses a snicker. I stand up and race to the door, sliding it back.

"I thought it was open," Mr. Buckley says.

Lammie Pie rushes into the family room, swipes the empty

plastic cups from Mr. Buckley's hands, and places them aside. She grabs her towel and dabs his face and shirt. "You need some dry clothes," she mumbles. He wraps an unsteady arm around her shoulders and motions toward the staircase. "I have some shirts and shorts upstairs," he says.

Elizabeth meets them on the stairway and slithers past. She finds me in the kitchen, dumping the empty cups into the garbage beside the sink.

"What happened?" she asks.

"Mr. Buckley walked into the sliding glass door," I say, matter-of-factly. "He thought it was open."

"Really?"

Someone has started the BBQ grill. Charcoal smoke and the smell of chicken wafts through the window. Elizabeth clutches her stomach. "I'm hungry," she says.

"You have a plate of food outside," I remind her.

"But I want chicken," she says. Her gaze wanders up the stairs. "Where did Mom go?"

"To help Mr. Buckley change."

Elizabeth's eyes widen. "You mean she gets to see him naked?"

"I don't think he's that wet." I turn around and lean against the counter. I remember my father warning me to watch my sisters, to filter everything for them through my eyes and ears and words. "Listen. Would you rather be here than home with Dad?"

She nods.

"Then don't ask too many questions, okay? Mom will get nervous and we'll have to leave like we always do." It is easier to shut Elizabeth up than it is to make up stories about the adults' behavior. I'm not as socially precocious as Cynthia is, and I'm not as good a liar as my father is. I'm just as scared and confused as Elizabeth, but I'm not allowed to show it to anyone.

By the time we step outside again, a cloud of smoke drifts over the pool. Cynthia greets us. Elizabeth picks at her potato salad and eyes the BBQ chicken. I pull up another chair to sit beside Cynthia and wonder how much longer we will get to stay. Already the sun is sinking fast behind the fence. I pretend to not pay attention to what is happening around us: adults getting drunk and smoking cigarettes and splashing in the pool and telling jokes and stories I do not understand. The less I know, the better I feel. Squinting, I study the sky, how its delicate blue melts into a purple stain in the west. I think about the possibility of taking a painting class when school starts to add color to my drawings. The Chihuahua scampers around our legs, searching for scraps of food, but there is nothing to eat. By the time the dark-purple stain soaks up the rest of the sky, the BBQ chicken is ready. Elizabeth squeezes first in line and eats two plates full. Cynthia nibbles at a chicken wing, having no room for much food, having snacked here and there all afternoon. I grab a plate for myself and while a man asks if I want a thigh or a breast, I gaze up at the house, scanning all the curtained windows upstairs, wondering where Lammie Pie is and what she could be doing. My interest, however, is fleeting, for part of me wants to remain ignorant of my mother's whereabouts and doings.

"Thigh or breast?" the man asks again.

"White or dark," a woman says, further clarifying the question.

"White," I say.

"That's the breast," the man says, placing a thick slab of glazed chicken on my plate.

I hunker down next to my sisters and eat. A few moments before we are done, a shadow passes over us and Cynthia smiles up at it.

I turn around and see my mother standing in a summer frock, a light frilly thing with tiny flowers. Her bare shoulders gleam like full moons. Her brown curls cling against her smile. She is not the mother I have grown up with, the shy, meek woman who cowered behind a layer of fat. This woman is strangely confident and beautiful.

"Ready to go?" Lammie Pie asks.

She touches my shoulder. A bolt of electricity shudders through me. I squint up at her, feeling like Sleeping Beauty awakened after one hundred years. Everything has changed.

"Aren't you going to eat?" Elizabeth asks. "The chicken's good."

"It's getting late and I'm not hungry," Lammie Pie says. "Finish up and we'll leave, okay?" She turns and motions toward the house. "I'll be inside watching TV."

I bite my lower lip and refrain from asking any questions. I still want to believe my mother is perfect, as perfect as the women I spend hours drawing. I don't want to know if she's capable of creating chaos like the women in the daytime soap operas I watch with my father. "Don't drink. Don't smoke. Don't flirt," Chee tells my sisters and me. "It will only lead to trouble." I don't want my mother to end up in trouble. I don't know what would happen to my sisters and me without her to protect us. I gaze up at the sky pricked with stars and feel my eyes sting with sudden tears.

Cynthia stares at me and asks, "What's wrong with you?"

"Nothing," I lie, wiping a quick hand over my eyes. I tear into my chicken with fierce teeth.

"Nuh-uh," Cynthia teases. "Something's the matter. What is it?"

I fake a shiver. "It's getting cold," I say. "Aren't you cold?"

"Not really." Cynthia eyes me. "You aren't going to tell us, are you? You're going to keep it a secret."

Elizabeth stares up at me, expectantly. I want to tell her not to worry, I'll be all right, but honestly, I don't know anymore. I am in between two worlds and suddenly aware I fit into neither one of them. Elizabeth stares at me with wide-eyed innocence and Cynthia smirks at me with cynical understanding. My stomach clenches like a tight fist, and I set my half-eaten chicken breast aside. I am nauseous. Maybe, I think, my father is right. We should not have come to the party.

Elizabeth sits on the ledge of the pool and kicks her feet back and forth through the water, gnawing on chicken bones. Someone has found the Chihuahua. "He's not himself tonight," the dog's owner says, cupping the tipsy dog in his affectionate hands. "Seems a little lost and spacey."

"Maybe he's drunk like the rest of us," a woman says, giggling.

Everyone bursts into good-humored laughter, and Cynthia turns to me with a knowing smile.

"Time to go," Lammie Pie says, ushering us into house. "Your father called and he's worried about us."

"Why'd he call?" Elizabeth asks.

Lammie Pie sighs. "He thought we'd be home for dinner."

"But it's after eight o'clock," I say, spying the glow-in-the-dark hands of my watch. "Why didn't he call earlier?"

Lammie Pie shakes her head and tugs us inside. We wander through the family room to use the bathroom and rinse our hands. Cynthia squints at her reflection in the mirror. "I hope I don't freckle," she says, examining her small nose.

"Don't worry," I reassure her. "You never have before."

"C'mon, let's go," Elizabeth says, tugging my hand. "You don't want Dad to get any angrier than he already is."

"Why should he be angry?" Cynthia demands. "He was invited. He could have come. But he decided to stay home. It was his choice. Why should he be angry about it?"

"He cooked dinner for us," Elizabeth explains.

"So what? He didn't have to. He could have napped all afternoon like he usually does. Or washed his car. Or read his magazines."

I unlock the bathroom door and lead my sisters to the family room where Lammie Pie curls up on the sofa beside Mr. Buckley who has changed into a short-sleeved button down shirt and denim shorts. He stretches one arm along the back of the sofa, his fingers dangling just above Lammie Pie's bare shoulder. They are watching the flickering images on the TV. When they notice us, Mr. Buckley gets up to hug us good-bye. He bends down to squeeze us, and I notice he genuinely wants to wish us well, not feel us up like Chee's boss and coworkers always do.

At the front door, he turns to me as I stand beside my mother and asks, "Has anyone told you that you look just like your mother? You could almost be twins."

I sneak a peek at my mother. We are the same height and shape. We share the same dazzling smile and long, tapered fingers and nervous laugh, but that's where the similarities end. I am not my mother. I am someone else.

Lammie Pie seems to sense my distance from her. She smiles coyly at Mr. Buckley and teases, "We can't be twins. Angela tans. I burn."

Mr. Buckley chuckles. "See you Monday, Margaret. Glad you could come." He waves to us.

"We had fun," Lammie Pie says. "Thank you for inviting us."

The smile lingers on Lammie Pie's face long after we have filed into the van and driven down the street. She hums to herself without turning on the radio. Instead of turning on the air conditioning, a habit Chee has, she rolls down the window and lets a cool evening breeze play with her hair. The frown lines around her lips have dissolved and the wrinkles at the corners of her eyes have crinkled into silent laughter. She looks younger, as young as she does in the black-and-white photographs Chee has shown us from when they were dating eighteen years ago.

"Did you have fun?" she asks.

"I had fun," Elizabeth says. "The pool was nice and the chicken was good."

"Did you see the Chihuahua?" Cynthia asks. "It got drunk. That was the best part." She pauses, and I think she wants to add: except for Mr. Buckley walking into the sliding glass door, but she closes her mouth and sits back with a silly smile on her lips.

"I'm glad you had fun," Lammie Pie says. "Because if your father is as angry as I imagine he is, then it will be the last party we're allowed to go to."

I don't care. I don't like parties. Neither the quiet decorum of a Chinese banquet nor the rollicking laughter of a company picnic. I prefer solitude.

Cynthia chokes. "No more parties?"

Elizabeth's face tenses with resistance. "Why do we always have to listen to him?"

No one answers her question.

Lammie Pie's smile washes away. Her faded blue eyes seem tired and sad.

Silence swells to fill the van with an achy longing none of us seems to understand.

10: Broken China Doll

My sisters and I get out of the van as the garage door rattles down, enveloping us in darkness except for a spatter of fluorescent light. We step into the orange kitchen with Lammie Pie behind us. We flick on the light. The smell of greasy chicken lingers in the air. Our buoyant steps halt like stalled laughter when we hear the creaking floorboards in the hallway, the slap of flip-flops on the linoleum in the foyer. His shadow elongates across the dining room table before we glimpse his six-foot frame shouldering the doorway. His thick lips straighten into a tight line across his golden-brown skin.

"Sorry we're late," Lammie Pie says, her smile dissolving like sugar in iced tea.

"Why didn't you call?" Chee asks. "I made dinner."

"We ate at the party," Cynthia says.

"Barbeque chicken," says Elizabeth. "It was yummy. I had three pieces."

"I made chicken, too," Chee says. "Chinese chicken."

My sisters and I hold our breaths. Our darting glances balance the tightrope of tension between Chee and Lammie Pie. For a long moment, no one speaks.

"You're wearing different clothes," Chee says, sweeping his gaze across the summer frock that clings to Lammie Pie's sharp curves. He stares at her cleavage above the lacy neckline, at the slit in her skirt revealing a flash of milky-white thigh. "I've never seen that dress. Did you make it?"

"No, I bought it. I don't have time to sew anymore. Not since I've been working."

"You work only part-time," Chee sneers, the cut-glass clarity of his statement slices through her excuse, leaving a clean wound.

Lammie Pie winces. "I was supposed to quit after the strike, remember? But you said to work a little bit longer. Well, it's been a few years longer."

"Someone has to pay for Cynthia's dance lessons."

"Leave her out of this," Lammie Pie snaps. "I'm tired of you blaming the girls, especially when it's not their fault."

There are two exits from the kitchen: through the foyer and through the living room. Chee blocks the entry to the foyer. We slide our feet toward the living room.

"Where you going?" Chee demands, his gaze striking us back into the room. "No one said you could leave."

"Let them go, Dave. It's between us."

"I'm not talking to you, Lammie Pie."

"But *I am* talking to you."

Chee nods, releasing us. We scatter like balls on a pool table. Cynthia disappears into the family room addition behind the folding Chinese partition that gives her a semiprivate bedroom. Elizabeth skips down to the end of the hallway to her pink-and-red room. I slip into the cool blue of my room and sit cross-legged on my bed, straining to listen.

"Is that alcohol I smell?" Chee asks.

"So what if I had a few drinks," Lammie Pie says. "It was only beer."

"You drank in front of the children?"

"Everyone was drinking. Even the dog was drunk."

"You let the kids drink?"

"Don't be ridiculous. Of course not. I'm not a bad mother."

"Just a drunk mother."

"I'm not drunk!"

"Keep your voice down," Chee warns. "The neighbors might hear you. You don't want them to know, do you?"

"Know what?" Lammie Pie demands. "That my husband is a control freak who's upset because he can't control me anymore?"

"I'm not a control freak." Chee tries to modulate his voice against bristling anger. "I'm just asking you to be more responsible in front of our children."

"Look who's talking!" Feet shuffle from the kitchen into the foyer. Something thumps against my wall. The papers on my bulletin board flutter. I jump. "Gambler! Thief! Hypocrite!"

A moment of silence flows into Lammie Pie's breathless whisper. "You can't say anything, can you? Because it's true."

Chee's voice is stern. "Just because I fail doesn't mean you have to."

"I didn't fail. It was a party. I had a few drinks. I relaxed. The girls swam in the pool and ate chicken. They were fine. They didn't see anything worse than what you've shown them—renting movies about runaway kids who end up as porn actresses, driving through the red-light district, showing them *Playboy*."

"That's different," Chee says. "I'm educating them against the evil out there. When Elizabeth says she wants to run away, I have to show her how her life will be like. That's why I showed them that movie. And Angela just happened to be in the car when that prostitute approached me. It's not like I asked her for anything. And they have to know the push-ups I make them do will give them nice breasts."

"Lies and excuses, every single one!" Lammie Pie's keys jingle. The kitchen door snaps open and the garage door rattles up.

"Where you going?" Chee demands.

"Out." There is a pregnant pause before Lammie Pie adds, "Kiss the girls good-bye from me."

"You can't leave." Chee's flip-flops slap against the linoleum like a mad dancer.

"Oh, yes, I can. Watch me."

The van's engine rumbles down the drive. For a long moment, there is silence. The kitchen door clicks shut. The hall light flicks on and footsteps pad down the hall. Chee glances into my dark bedroom. I clamber off my bed, afraid of being reprimanded for sitting on the mattress, making it lumpy, wearing it out. But Chee lifts his hand and says, "It's okay. You stay sitting." He steps into the room, perches on the edge of the bed, folds his hands between his knees, and stares at the scarlet carpet.

"What happened?" I ask, although I already know.

"Your mama left." I can't see his eyes, but I can hear the tears in his voice.

Briefly, I consider reaching out to him, touching his shoulder, pulling him into my arms, letting him cry, but I don't. I can't comfort him after he has caused my mother so much misery.

He stares at the carpet, unmoving. Not even his eyes blink.

It is almost nine o'clock. Chee has not scolded us for not brushing our teeth or changing into our pajamas or saying our prayers or going to bed. He sits at his desk in his bedroom staring at the wall. Sometimes Elizabeth will peek at him from the doorway of her room to see if he has moved. Other times, Cynthia paces the length of the hall, trying to get his attention. Once, I call out his name, first in Chinese, then in English. But he just sits and stares. Finally, as the clock swiftly approaches ten, my sisters and I resign ourselves to our evening rituals. We slip under the covers of our beds and pretend to sleep.

Once the lights are out, Chee wanders up and down the hall, pacing like an expectant father in a maternity ward. I imagine he lifts the curtain in his bedroom window facing the street every time a car rolls by, hoping it might be her. I imagine each time it isn't, he sighs. I toss and turn, trying to forget what I can't help but remember: Lammie Pie walking with Mr. Buckley up the stairs, her arm around his drunken shoulders. I remember sitting beside the pool nibbling on BBQ chicken and glancing up every now and then to the second-story windows, hoping to glimpse her laughing silhouette or silent shadow, but seeing nothing through the closed curtains, not even movement from inside. I remember listening to Cynthia tell us about the drunken Chihuahua and how no one cared what happened to the poor dog because they were too busy slapping back beers and soaking in the last bits of sun. I remember tilting my head back and gazing at the bruised sky as the colors changed from blue and gold to red and purple and black.

Chee startles me out of my reverie when he sits at the foot of my bed and cups my knee through the bedding. I open my eyes and gasp. He raises a finger to his lips. "Shhh! You close your eyes, you go to sleep, you listen to me right now. About your mother. How she was bad today. Don't you ever talk like that when you're married. Okay? Don't you ever walk out on your husband. Okay? Don't be selfish. Don't be stubborn. Stay and work it out. Okay?"

I close my eyes and nod, folding my hands over my breasts, as if it might add another layer of protection against me and him. I want to tell him I don't blame my mother, but it would be a half-truth because part of me does blame her for not taking my sisters and me with her, for abandoning us to this man who calls himself an exemplary husband and father, a man my mother knows is a liar, a thief, a womanizer, and a hypocrite.

So, I keep my eyes closed and listen to Chee prattle on and on about the sins of my mother. "She's disrespectful," he says. "No wonder Cynthia doesn't respect me. She doesn't eat what I make. No wonder she's so skinny. She doesn't call to let me know she's running late. It's all Joanne's fault. That woman poisoned Lammie Pie, made her into someone no one knows anymore."

Unlike my father, I have viewed Joanne as a cautionary tale, not a threat of liberation for my mother. I have overheard my mother speaking with Joanne on the phone about their envy of housewives who can fold laundry and watch TV or shop for new clothes while their children are safe in school.

I want to bolt upright in my bed and tell my father these things, but I clutch my thoughts and feelings at the base of my throat until they dissolve back into my body and swirl through my blood making me sweat. I want to throw off the covers, but my father sits on them, pinning me to the bed. My only escape is to pretend to sleep.

My silence breeds suspicion. Chee shakes my knee and asks, "You listening?"

I blink a few times and pretend to rub sleep from my eyes. "Huh?" I ask.

"Don't be like your mother, you hear? Don't talk to single women when you're married. You go to work and come home to your kids, okay? Don't dress in sexy clothes or talk to other men, okay? You wear modest dresses that fall below the knee and do not smile when men try to flirt with you, okay? You be a good girl and do not go to parties where people get drunk in front of children. You stay home and be a good wife, a good mother, okay?"

"Yes, sir," I mumble.

He squeezes my knee one last time before he stands up and wanders into the next room to talk to Elizabeth, to repeat what he has already said to me. Later, he wanders down the hall into the family room partition where Cynthia sleeps.

"She can leave if she wants to," Cynthia says, her voice rising. "You don't own her. She's her own person."

"Aiyaah! She's not. She's my wife. She's supposed to stay for better or worse."

"Yeah? Well, this is worse than worse. This is hell."

"How dare you speak that way to your father? Shame on you. You be nothing when you grow up. No man want you. You'll have to work the rest of your days and you'll be all alone like Joanne."

"I don't want to get married if getting married means living like you and Mom do," Cynthia hisses. "I'd rather be single and all alone. I'd rather enjoy myself."

The conversation ends. Chee storms out of the room muttering to himself. He slams the door of his bedroom. I wonder how Cynthia could be so bold and not be thrown out. Maybe Chee is afraid she would not return. Maybe he fears we will all leave him, one by one, until he is alone. Maybe—

But I tire of speculations. I roll over and clutch the radio Chow dog to my breasts, listening to the faint whisperings of Night Beat against the agitated rhythm of my heart and try to fall asleep.

Sunday, Monday, Tuesday. We do not see or hear from Lammie Pie. By Wednesday, everyone thinks the worst. She is missing. She has been kidnapped. She has been raped and murdered. We start to eat meals without stealing furtive glances at the phone hanging on the orange wall in the kitchen. We start to omit her name from our evening prayers. We slowly erase her from our life.

Except Cynthia. She talks about her. At dinner, Cynthia asks, "Who will drive me to dance class, Dad?"

"I will tonight. But tomorrow, you must find a ride. I'll be at work."

The evening news blares from the TV. Cynthia reaches for the knob and turns it off. She points to Lammie Pie's vacant seat. "See this?" she asks. "This is all your fault. None of this would have happened if you'd just been nice to Mom once in a while, if you treated her like other men do."

"What other men?"

"The men in the bank who bring her flowers or take her to lunch. The men at the party who said she was beautiful. The men who make her smile and laugh. You should learn to be a little like those men."

"I am better than those men," Chee says, placing his fork against his plate. "I mean what I say. Those men don't."

"Just like you mean what you say to the women in the checkout line?" Cynthia asks. She reaches across the dining room table and grabs Elizabeth's hand, palm up, and pretends to be Chee. "Here's one for your mother, and here's one for your sister, and here's one for you, baby doll." She winks.

Chee pulls his face into a frown. "That's not funny."

The phone rings. Cynthia bolts up to get it, but Chee beats her to it. "Hello," he says, in his deep, husky voice.

Every muscle in his face creases into a smile. He cups the receiver with his palm and whispers to us, "It's Lammie Pie."

We glance around the table and hold each other's hands. Silently, we pray he will say the right thing and bring her back to us.

"Where are you?" Chee asks. "When are you coming back? Yes, she's here. Okay."

Chee hands the phone to me. "Your mother wants to speak with you."

I am surprised. I glance at my sisters, who stare back at me. My stomach clenches with dreadful anticipation. I wonder what Lammie Pie wants to say to me that she could not say to anyone else. When I pick up the receiver, my voice is hoarse. "Hello, Mom."

"Angela, I need you to tell me the truth." My mother's rapid-fire speech catches me off guard. "I can't ask Elizabeth. She's too young and she doesn't know any better. I can't ask Cynthia. She hates your father and she'll say anything to make him look bad. But you I can trust. So, tell me, how are you and your sisters? Is Chee being good to you or is he up to his old tricks?"

I glance at my father who sits at the head of the table, staring at me. I open the garage door and step outside into the dank darkness and close the door as far as the chord will allow. Sitting on the rug draped over the cement step between the washer and furnace, I whisper, "We're okay. We miss you. Dad says it's all our fault that you're gone. That you'd still be here if we were good enough."

"Up to his old tricks, I see." She pauses, as if she is either listening to another conversation or thinking of the right words to say. "It's not your fault or your sisters' fault, okay? I don't want any of you thinking that. It's between your father and me. Don't tell him, but I'm staying at Grandpa and Grandma's house for as long as they'll have me."

"When are you coming back?"

"I don't know."

A bit of anger catches flame in my voice. My words shoot out like sparks. "*Are* you coming back?"

"I don't know."

My heartbeat races. My palms sweat. I start to jabber. "You *have* to come back. You can't leave us with him. Cynthia has no one to take her to dance lessons. And Elizabeth whimpers all night like a lost puppy."

The silence crackles between us. I wonder what she is thinking, if she is thinking anything at all. Or if she has given up completely, abandoned us to save herself like the women in the soap operas who change their names and start a new life as someone else.

When she finally speaks, she sounds far away, as if she's talking from another country, not Grandpa and Grandma's house. "Joanne's husband used to beat her," she says. "What your father does is worse.

None of our bruises show. We have to hide our pain, pretend we're happy."

My anger has melted into tears. My voice trembles and breaks. "I thought you *were* happy. You were smiling at the picnic."

"But I'm not happy at home."

"Nobody is," I tell her. "Not even Dad."

"Something has to change," she tells me. "We can't go on with the same bullshit."

"You swore! I can't believe you swore."

"I used to swear a lot before I met your father. I used to hang out at bars after work. I dated lots of men. I'm not as innocent as you think I am."

"I don't want to hear this," I tell her. "You're breaking my heart." I stalk back into the kitchen and hand the phone to my father. I bolt down the hallway to my bedroom and slam the door. The award certificates on my bulletin board flutter like wings. I sink down at the foot of my bed and sob. *There is no happily-ever-after*, I think. *All those fairy tales are lies. Pretty lies.* On my hands and knees, I crawl over to my desk, open the top drawer, and pull out my drawings. I start to rip them up, one by one, and toss them on the blood-red carpet. But when I get to the last picture, the one of Cinderella losing her glass slipper on the steps of the palace, I stop. We have both lost something.

I hug the picture to my chest and rock back and forth until my father bangs on the door and flings it open.

"Aiyaah!" he shouts. "What did she say?"

"She's not coming home," I tell him. "She doesn't love us anymore. She wants to start a new life." The last part is just speculation, but at the moment I say it, it feels true, as real as the rough paper crinkled against my skin.

My father points to the flakes of paper scattered on the carpet. "What's this?"

"My drawings."

"Aiyaah! You don't want. You recycle. Understand?"

I burst into tears. *How can he think of practical things at a time like this?*

Elizabeth sneaks into my bedroom after my father is gone and wraps her chubby arms around my neck to snuggle with me. She's soft and warm, as cuddly as my mother was when she was overweight and silently suffering. I miss my mother. I want her to come back and rescue us.

I stroke Elizabeth's fine, long hair. She glances up at me with her wide brown eyes and says, "Dad said Mom's not coming back. I need a mommy. Will you be my new mommy?"

A wave of sadness threatens to topple me, and I squeeze Elizabeth tighter to brace myself against the current of tears that start to flow. *I'm not ready to be a mother*, I think. *I can't even take care of myself.* But, as I cradle her in my arms, I whisper, "Yes."

On Thursday afternoon, Lammie Pie calls again. Cynthia answers the phone. They talk for a few minutes before Cynthia rests the receiver on the kitchen counter and goes into our parents' bedroom to find Chee. He is sleeping on top of the bedspread, snoring. She nudges his feet. "Mom's on the phone. She wants to talk to you."

"Huh? Oh!" He sits up and scrambles for the phone beside his bed. He picks it up and says, "Hullo?" in his half-awake voice.

We stand around the phone in the kitchen and listen. Cynthia presses the receiver to her ear and we press our ears to her head, trying to snatch a random word or two. We hold our breaths, hoping no one will know we are trespassing on their privacy.

Only Cynthia has heard the entire conversation. When she hangs up the receiver, she whispers jubilantly, "She's coming home."

A wave of relief washes over us. We jump up and down and clap our hands.

"When?" I ask.

"Tonight."

We get ready for bed early and sit in the living room and fold our clothes and put them away in the proper drawers. We straighten the house and make sure the kitchen floor is swept. We haven't cleaned the house so thoroughly since Dad's mother, Mah-Mah, came to stay with us years ago. When we walk past the refrigerator, our reflections gleam back at us. We smile and giggle like girls at a slumber party.

The garage door rattles up at a quarter to eight. Chee hobbles down the hall. "She's here," he says.

We sit on the sofa with our feet dangling. We glance at the garage door, waiting for it to swing back, for Mom to step inside, to rescue us.

We hear them before we see them. Chee steps inside first, holding the door for Lammie Pie. Our mother steps inside. Her brown curls fall against her glowing white face. She's sporting a new dress, the color of a purple violet. She flashes a smile at us. There is an otherworldly quality to her, a distinct look none of us has seen before, a look we cannot name. She bends to embrace Cynthia who runs up to her like a long lost friend stepping off an airplane. Elizabeth clings to her knees, stammering, "I have my old mommy back!" I stand beside them, watching, waiting for my turn. When she releases my sisters, I step into her arms and hold her so tightly she begs for me to please let go.

"You're hurting my neck," she says.

As soon as I step back, the tears start to flow. The words choke out of my mouth. "I thought you abandoned us."

"I needed time to think, that's all," she says, as if she has just returned from a planned retreat, not gone missing for five days.

I am torn. Part of me wants to hit her, throw a water pitcher at her, scream at her, tell her how I really feel. But the other half wants to welcome her home.

Lammie Pie studies me. "I see you've taken good care of your sisters."

My voice wobbles. "Elizabeth asked me to be her new mommy."

Lammie Pie's face crumbles.

"We thought you left forever."

She presses her lips together and stares at me like I'm an impostor taking her place and she's the one rightfully angry, not me.

"I didn't create this family," I tell her. "I shouldn't have to be the one to keep it from falling apart."

"No one's asking you to," she says, struggling to keep her voice even. "I'm home now. You can go back to being a kid."

"How can I?" I ask. "I have responsibilities."

"Your only responsibility is to respect my wishes," she says. Her gaze sweeps across me and my sisters. "Go to bed. I'm in charge now."

I gape at her in disbelief. If she sees my face, she does not comment. Instead, she pulls my father aside and says, "We need to talk." She grabs his hand, leads him down the hallway and into their bedroom, and closes and locks the door.

Instead of going to bed like our mother asked, my sisters and I slump on the carpet and turn on the TV. Cynthia says, "I haven't seen this commercial before." Elizabeth looks at me and asks, "Why did you yell at Mommy?"

"Aren't you mad at her for leaving?" I ask.

Elizabeth lies on her stomach and kicks her feet in the air. "She's home. It's all better now."

"How can everything be all better just because she comes home?"

"Shh!" Cynthia says, raising a finger to her lips. "The movie is starting."

I stare at them for a moment, then decide to obey my mother. I stand up and announce, "I don't care if either of you get into trouble. I'm going to bed."

Their blank gazes follow me to the edge of the living room before they swing back to the flickering images on the TV.

11: VISIT TO MAH-MAH

The day after Lammie Pie returns, Chee's union goes on strike. Whenever Chee is not picketing, he is home. After one week of no work and no pay, Lammie Pie decides to not risk an extended loss of income for the family and asks Mr. Buckley if she can work full-time. With the financial burden shifted from my father to my mother, I notice a change in the dynamics at home. My father sleeps more. My mother comes home at six and makes dinner and ushers us to bed as quickly as possible. She tries to stay up to sew, but falls asleep before the evening soaps start.

By the third week, Chee assumes the household responsibilities. He mixes rice and leftovers in a saucepan, adds an egg and soy sauce, and calls the meal fried rice. My sisters miss our mother and her fresh cooking. Sometimes Chee stares out the kitchen window, waiting for the van to pull into the drive, just like Elizabeth used to sit by the kitchen window, waiting for Cynthia to come home from school so they could play dolls. We think Chee misses Lammie Pie as much as we do.

My mother is so busy working that my birthday passes without a homemade cake.

A week later, the strike ends. Lammie Pie is relieved. She can return to working only part-time. But something has permanently changed at home. Chee doesn't argue as much with our mother, knowing she could walk away and support the family, if she wanted to. Lammie Pie has gained a new respect and appreciation for our father as the breadwinner and leader of the family. She still defers to him on certain issues, but there is deliberateness to her submission and a quiet contentment in her ability to return to her evening sewing after a month's absence.

Two weeks before school starts, Chee decides we need to visit his mother, Mah-Mah, in San Francisco.

"I don't want to go," Cynthia whines. "All we've done this summer is travel."

"You have to go," Chee says, sliding open the side door of the van. "Mah-Mah give you money. You can buy clothes."

Cynthia climbs into the van.

"I don't care about money," Elizabeth says. "Do I have to go?"

"Mah-Mah give you something good to eat," Chee says. "Maybe red-bean cake."

Elizabeth climbs into the van.

"I don't care about money or food," I tell Chee. "I just want to stay home and relax. Watch TV for a change."

Chee purses his lips. "You can watch TV any time. They have reruns. But Mah-Mah is getting old," he says. "Someday she won't be with us. You visit her now while she's alive, understand?"

I cross my arms over my chest and refuse to move.

Lammie Pie rolls down her window and says, "Chee feels guilty because none of you got to meet his father. He was already dead before you were born."

"He's only going to get money and food," I tell Lammie Pie. "He doesn't care about anything else."

Chee points at the van. "Get in."

Lammie Pie pleads with me with her eyes.

I climb into the van. Chee shuts the door.

We are silent during the trip. In Chinatown, Chee swerves into a loading zone and shouts for us to get out. We wait on the curb while he properly parks the van. Lammie Pie clutches her leather purse to her chest. Cynthia presses her nose against a picture window full of plastic shoes in vibrant, sunny blues and pinks and yellows and greens. "Look," she says, pointing to a sandal. "Those are rhinestones."

In a jewelry-store window, we see different shades of jade and long chains of braided gold. "Light green is best," I say, remembering what Mah-Mah once told Lammie Pie. "And only 24K gold will do."

"Look at that ivory elephant," Cynthia says, pointing. "I want one just like it for Christmas."

Chee hustles up the block, weaving through tourists, his keys jangling from a chain hooked to his belt. He grabs Lammie Pie's elbow and steers her into the bakery. Within moments, Chee has paid for whatever is inside the three pink plastic bags. He carries two and hands one to Lammie Pie, who shifts her purse to the inside arm between her and Elizabeth and takes the plastic bag in her free hand. Chee points to the van parked down the street. Cynthia stops to linger at a storefront window full of traditional silk cheongsam dresses with frog closures at the Mandarin neck and thigh-high slits on either side. "It's just like the one Mom made for her wedding," Cynthia whispers.

I grab her hand and we hustle down the street squeezing past strangers who step on our toes. Chee waves for us to get into the van. "Aiyaah! Hurry!" Chee drives out of Chinatown.

A few hills up and over, we pull into the underground parking lot of Mah-Mah's apartment building. Sounds echo. The stale smell of stinking feet wafts up with the breeze. Lammie Pie brings one plastic bag with her, the others stay in the van. Chee shuffles over to the elevator. Elizabeth presses the button until it glows white. We stand beside the door and wait, listening to brakes screech at the light and the clanging bells of cable cars as they move up and down the street.

Mah-Mah's apartment is located on the second floor. Chee places a finger over his thick lips, indicating for us to be quiet. "Old people live here," he says, motioning to the open doors that allow a peek into a foreign world of ancient Chinese people playing mah jong, reading newspapers, or drinking tea and gossiping in Cantonese.

Chee knocks on an orange door at the end of the hall. A small woman peeks beneath the golden security chain before a smile of recognition stretches across her brown face. She closes the door and releases the chain and then pulls the door open, bowing and smiling. Chee bends down to kiss her cheek. Lammie Pie follows, giving her a hug. I usher Cynthia and Elizabeth ahead of me. They wrap their arms around her and give a squeeze. Mah-Mah grabs my shoulders and looks me in the eyes and says, "You taller than me." She glances down at her embroidered silk house slippers and at my leather flats just to make sure neither of us is cheating. When she smiles and pulls me close for a hug, she smells of moth balls and ginger. Her skin is cool and strangely smooth. She wears the same dark-blue housecoat she has worn for years, a sapphire-blue embroidered silk cheongsam. Her knees barely move as she pads down the wide hall and into the kitchen area. Elizabeth and Cynthia flop on the blue-and-yellow brocade sofa and try to glance past the bookcase that serves as a barrier between the dining room table and the double bed. Lammie Pie clutches her purse to her chest. Mah-Mah motions to the plastic-coated table, but Lammie Pie just glances at her odd waving gestures and refuses to move. Finally, Mah-Mah grabs the purse and plays tug-of-war until Lammie Pie surrenders it. Triumphantly, Mah-Mah sets the leather purse on the center of the table and says, "Sit there," pulling out a chair for Lammie Pie, who obediently sits, staring at her purse.

Mah-Mah turns on the stove and boils water for tea. Chee says, "No, Mah-Mah, we go out for dinner." He nods for us to give Mah-Mah the gift he bought at the bakery. We gape at him with open mouths. Chee plucks the pink plastic bag from the floor and hands it to Mah-Mah. "We bring dessert," Chee says. "Your favorite. Black-bean cake."

Mah-Mah sets it on the table beside Lammie Pie's purse. She does not open the bag or peek at its contents, but returns to the stove to tend to the water. Chee purses his lips and rustles through the bag, removing a pink box. With his key, he cuts the string, lifts the cover, and removes a white, flaky cake. Carefully, with one hand beneath the cake-carrying hand, he struts to the stove and bends down to offer Mah-Mah a bite. She shakes her head, pursing her lips in the same fashion Chee always does, and says in her halting English, "You feed kids."

"We have our own box in the van," Chee explains. "This one for you."

Mah-Mah pushes Chee's arm aside like it is a swinging door. She sidles over to my sisters and me who sit shoulder to shoulder and knee to knee on the small couch. "You hungry?" she asks, handing us an odd-shaped yellow, pink, and green melon.

"What is it?" I ask, fondling the smooth, hard skin.

"Mango," Chee says. "It's a fruit. Like oranges."

Mah-Mah opens a brown paper bag and places it on the floor. She lifts the mango from my hands and peels the skin with her nails and drops the skin into the brown paper bag. The mango's yellowish flesh smells sickly sweet. With her fingers, she offers us each a piece. I sniff the strange odor and bite into the stringy fruit. It tastes awful. My lips pucker and my mouth swells. I do not want to chew; I do not want to swallow. Grabbing a tissue from the side table, I pretend to blow my nose. The slick yellow wedge slips out of my mouth and into the tissue. I wrap it up and wait for the opportunity to get rid of the fruit permanently.

Mah-Mah offers me another slice. I shake my head and say, "I'm full."

"She saving room for dinner, right, Angela?" Chee says, nodding.

I want to tell him I hate mangos, but I just nod and fake a smile.

Cynthia and Elizabeth have somehow managed to eat their mangos. Lammie Pie sits patiently at the table observing each of us.

"I have to go to the bathroom," I say.

"You all go," Chee says, ushering us down the hall and to the left. "Lammie, you help them, okay?"

We squeeze into the oversized bathroom with its shower and tub enclosure, toilet, mirror, and sink. Once inside, I unwrap the tissue and plunk the mango into the toilet and flush.

"What was that?" Elizabeth asks.

"Nothing," I lie.

"You didn't eat the fruit?" Cynthia asks.

Chee raps on the closed door. "You almost ready?"

"Just a minute," I say.

When we are done, we follow Chee back into the kitchen area. Mah-Mah has changed into a simple dress and grabbed her black wool coat with the mink collar and matching mink cap. Her black rubber-soled shoes remind me of nurses' slippers.

"Ready?" Mah-Mah asks us.

In the parking garage, Chee helps lift Mah-Mah into the front seat. Lammie Pie sits in my chair and I sit in the back beside Elizabeth. We help Chee back up, telling him when he is too close to the concrete post or the red compact car waiting to pull in.

Once on the streets, Chee relaxes. He coasts up and down the streets of San Francisco and parallel parks near the Grand Palace Restaurant. We walk uphill, Cynthia and I holding Mah-Mah's hands. She shuffles with us, carrying her big black purse around her wrist. "You nice girls," she says to us. Elizabeth holds Lammie Pie's hand. Chee hustles in front of us, hurrying to the restaurant to secure us the best table.

The streets smell of seafood and salt. Although the fog has burned off, there is a chilly undercurrent that rushes underneath our clothes. The soles of my shoes stick against the dirty pavement. Cynthia sneaks a glance at a roast duck hanging in a store window.

By the time we reach the restaurant, Chee is holding open the door and waving us inside. "Aiyaah! We got a table. Hurry! Hurry! Hurry!"

A waitress with braided black hair and heavy white makeup on her face leads us to the middle of the restaurant away from the hustle and bustle of the reception area and the hubbub of the kitchen. Her silk cheongsam shifts against the curves of her body as she walks. Chee smiles and says, "Thank you," in Cantonese. She smiles and nods, offering him a menu. Chee waves it away. "I already know what I order."

We pull back the black chairs with red-and-gold seat cushions and sit down around a circular table covered in a white tablecloth. The waitress places a steel pot with hot tea on the lazy Susan next to the Chinese condiments, hot mustard, and soy sauce.

Elizabeth removes a red napkin from the table and places it on her lap. Cynthia and I imitate her. We glance at Mah-Mah, who sits between Chee and Lammie Pie. She removes her coat and hat and hands them to Chee, who offers them to a waiter.

The restaurant is huge and noisy. Chopsticks click against china. Waiters weave in between tables carrying platters of exotic dishes. The air smells of ginger and garlic and sweet and sour sauce. Cynthia spins the lazy Susan. Elizabeth stares straight ahead as if she is afraid to move. Lammie Pie smiles quietly. Mah-Mah tilts her head when Chee talks, spewing a slew of sharp vowels and soft consonants.

Minutes later, a waiter places a bowl of wonton soup on the lazy Susan. With one hand, he scoops out the contents into white porcelain bowls and hands them to us. One by one, the other dishes arrive. Chee stops eating and starts piling food on Mah-Mah's plate. She holds out her hand and says, "No." Chee waits a moment, then slaps another spoonful of tomato-beef chow mein on Mah-Mah's plate. She starts to bicker with him in Cantonese, her words flying like fists against his face. He cowers, quietly absorbing the pummeling words until tears surface.

Cynthia nudges me with her foot. I lean toward her and she whispers, "He's going to cry."

I shake my head. Chee does not cry over anything. Once, when he was too harsh with me, demanding perfection over a spelling test when he could not pronounce the words correctly, he apologized for helping me fail. "From now on, Lammie Pie will help you with homework," he said. "I speak funny. You don't understand what words teacher says because you think of them like I say them. Incorrectly. I'm sorry." His brown eyes glistened, but tears did not streak his cheeks. I do not think they will tonight, either.

But Cynthia persists. "You can always tell how much the Chinese love you by how much they feed you," she says. "Or by how much money they give you."

I nod.

"If she doesn't eat his food, she's telling him she doesn't love him."

I lift my eyebrows, disbelieving.

Cynthia whispers, "Wait and see."

Mah-Mah scoots her chair back. She waves to a waiter to bring her coat and hat. Chee grabs her arms and pulls her down into her seat. His words are slow and soft. Mah-Mah yips at him. She shovels tomato-beef chow mein onto my plate, cashew chicken onto

Cynthia's plate, and motions to Elizabeth to slide her plate across the lazy Susan so she can dump her sautéed scallops on her plate.

Chee purses his lips. His brown eyes are moist.

Lammie Pie lowers her chopsticks and eyes Chee as if she is wondering what she can say or do to break up the argument and restore peace. But she does not speak the language. None of us do, except Chee. And, according to him, it is only a halting, baby-talk interpretation of the language that he converses in, a pathetic weapon in a fight with a powerful woman who wields her native tongue like a newly sharpened sword. Lammie Pie can only guess from the tone of their voices and the violence of their gestures what is being spoken. Her blue eyes are soft with an inexplicable sadness and sympathy. She looks caught between the impulse to hold Chee's hand and a natural resistance to interfere in a private matter between mother and son. I don't envy her position. For once, I am happy to be in observance, quietly eating, absorbing the light and laughter of the restaurant, the focus of the evening on someone other than me.

The waiter returns with Mah-Mah's coat and hat. Chee folds a ten-dollar bill into his hand and ushers him away. The waiter leaves with the coat and hat. Mah-Mah hits Chee's arm and yelps at him in her rapid-fire Cantonese.

After Chee has disposed of more money than he may have anticipated and after several attempts to retrieve her coat and hat, Mah-Mah succeeds in slipping into her coat and hat and shuffling to the front of the restaurant with Chee loping after her. Lammie Pie instructs the waiter to box up the leftovers and give her the bill immediately. The waiter bows. Within moments, he returns with the bill and several white folding boxes with metal handles. He scoops up the remaining food and expertly folds the tops. Lammie Pie hands the waiter the bill and a plastic MasterCard. She signs her name and leaves a sizable tip. Gathering the boxes into a plastic bag, she motions for us to follow her out of the restaurant. Elizabeth slips her greasy hand in mine and whispers, "Are we in trouble?"

"No," I say. "Dad is."

Outside, we look up and down the street, searching for them. Chee stands beside the van with his hands on Mah-Mah's shoulders.

Although he towers over her physically, she commands a strength that supersedes this world. Lammie Pie approaches them. Chee asks if she paid. She nods. Then, with surprising ease, Lammie Pie bends to Mah-Mah and says, "We'll take you home now."

Mah-Mah shakes her head and bats Chee's arms away. "I walk."

"It's very far," Lammie Pie says. "We'll drive you."

"I walk."

Lammie Pie opens the front door and places the bag on the floor between the two seats. She unlocks the remaining doors and says to us, "Get in."

My sisters and I hustle around the van, carefully observing the flow of traffic. We slide the door back and hurry inside. Lammie Pie tries to coax Mah-Mah into the van. She speaks to Mah-Mah in slow, patient words, repeating her requests. But Mah-Mah is stubborn, as stubborn as Chee, and she refuses to get in.

Mah-Mah begins to shuffle down the street, head held high, mink cap tilted back, a regal queen. Chee runs after her, shouting, begging, apologizing.

Lammie Pie slips inside the driver's seat and starts the engine.

"What are you doing?" Elizabeth asks.

"Driving away." Lammie Pie flicks the indicator and merges into traffic. "If they want to fight, they can fight."

"Are we going home?" Cynthia asks, grasping the back of Lammie Pie's seat. "Are we going to leave Dad here, too?"

Lammie Pie does not say anything. She steers through the hills, around tourist cluttered corners, and down one-way streets.

Before we leave Chinatown, I turn my head and glance out the back window. Chee continues to hustle after Mah-Mah, the urgency of his steps countering the steady pattering of her rubber-soled feet. I see them disappear.

I try to imagine a life without Chee, without his early-morning lectures, without his constant instruction, without his daily schedule written in black permanent-ink marker and taped to the closet door, without his stack of *Reader's Digest* and *Consumer Today* magazines stacked in the bathroom, without his monthly ledger locked in the top drawer of his desk mapping out our income and expenses, tracking every single penny earned and spent. I try to imagine a world without newspapers and manufacturers' coupons, without soap operas and afternoon naps punctuated with bleating snores, without rules and demands. I try to imagine what our family would be like without him to lead and guide us.

But I do not have to imagine very long. Lammie Pie has driven us back to Mah-Mah's apartment building. She parks the van in the garage and turns off the engine. She sits quietly in the front seat and waits.

"I thought we were going home," Cynthia says, a rough edge of disappointment in her voice.

Lammie Pie glances at her watch.

"We can still make it home," Cynthia says. "They won't miss us." Lammie Pie stares out the window at the stone wall and does not speak.

"It's our chance to escape," Cynthia says.

"I know what life is like without your father," Lammie Pie says. "I can't live without him and neither can you."

"That's a lie!" Cynthia slams her back against her seat and crosses her arms over her chest. "I don't believe you've fallen for a lie. I thought you were smarter than that."

"There are some things you won't understand till after you're grown and moved out. Until then, you will have to trust my judgment. You will have to abide by my decisions."

"You sound like Dad."

"Sometimes Dad is right."

"What if they fight all night and don't get home till tomorrow morning?"

"Then we'll sleep in the van. We've done it before."

Cynthia sighs.

A half hour later, they arrive, still bickering. "Stay here," Lammie Pie says. She steps out of the van and approaches them, tugging on Chee's shirtsleeve, urging him to come with us, to leave the poor old woman alone. But Chee is not finished arguing. He shakes his fist at Mah-Mah, who shakes her fist right back at him. They go back and forth imitating each other's frustration and anger, not getting anything resolved.

"I wonder what they're fighting about," I say.

"Probably the food," Cynthia says. "Chee thinks Mah-Mah doesn't love him. She thinks he's a fool."

"How do you know that for sure?" I ask, turning toward her.

Cynthia shrugs. "It's obvious, isn't it? Just look at them. You don't have to speak the language to understand human nature. Everyone wants to be loved, especially by one's parents. And Chee only has his mother left. His father died before we were born. So it's not like he has any options. She either loves him or he's unlovable. And because she won't eat his food or take his money, that makes him unlovable. And Chee wants everyone to like him. That's why he flirts with strange women and jokes with strange men. He wants everyone to be his friend, but he also wants no one to really know him. That would make him weak. And a man can't be weak."

I glance out the window. Chee is trying to bend down to hug his mother good-bye, but she just bats him away with her purse. Lammie Pie tugs him toward the van. He looks back longingly, then hunches his shoulders and slips into the passenger's seat. He turns to us. "You okay?" he asks.

"We're fine," I say. "How are *you*?"

He purses his lips and glances away.

Lammie Pie starts the engine and heads home. Once on the highway, she turns on the stereo. Music fills the space. Chee snaps off the stereo and begins to talk.

"I want you to know I love you," he says, turning to us. "I want you to know I think I'm very blessed to have three beautiful and healthy and talented girls."

"Then why do you always treat us like shit?" Cynthia asks.

"Don't curse." Chee's eyes flash with momentary anger. He presses his lips together and stares at the floor, as if regretting what he just said. When he speaks again, his voice is a caress. "I'm sorry if you feel that way. I'm only trying to raise you right."

"We aren't perfect," Cynthia says. "It's inhuman to think we'll ever be."

"Not inhuman," Chee says, glancing up at her. His brown eyes blaze. "You can always do better."

"Better? You're never happy with better. You want the best."

"Aiyaah! I don't expect too much. Just look at your room. It's a pigsty. You look at your sisters' rooms. They are neat. Especially Angela. Everything has its place. She knows where everything goes. She keeps it there, not all over the floor and bed and dressers like you do."

"Elizabeth hides toys under her bed."

"Hey, don't bring me into it!" Elizabeth shouts. "I don't want to fight."

"We aren't fighting," Chee says. "We're talking."

"You raise your voice, it's a fight," Cynthia says. "So, technically, you're wrong."

"I haven't raised my voice," Chee says.

"Liar!"

"I'm not lying."

Cynthia shakes her head. "I told Mom she should have left you. But she didn't."

Chee glances at Lammie Pie with a hint of new respect, then he returns his attention to us.

"I want you to know you're ungrateful," Chee says to Cynthia. "In China, you would have been drowned."

"I wish I had been. It would have been better than living with you."

Chee shouts, "Lammie Pie, stop! We let Cynthia out. Let her see how easy it is without us."

"You won't," Cynthia snaps. "You have a conscience."

Lammie Pie stares straight ahead and says, "Listen to your father or I will pull over."

"You're taking his side again," Cynthia says.

Lammie Pie flicks on the turn indicator.

Cynthia leans back in her chair and closes her mouth.

Chee resumes talking. "I just wanted to say I love you. That's all." He turns around.

I glance at Cynthia and Elizabeth. They both are silent.

"I love you, too, Dad," I say.

"Me, too," says Elizabeth.

Only Cynthia remains silent.

"I love you, too," says Lammie Pie.

I stare at Cynthia, waiting to see if she will say something, anything.

But she just frowns.

12: Back-to-School Blues

A week before school starts, Lammie Pie and I meet with a counselor to determine my class schedule. I have two electives, the counselor explains. He points to my grades. "You've already taken Spanish and chemistry," he says. "Maybe you want to take something fun this semester. Like electronics or woodshop."

"I want to take drawing and painting," I say.

Lammie Pie places her hand on the sign-up sheet. "She'll take typing and home economics."

On the ride home, I sulk. "I want to be a professional artist. How can I learn if I don't take classes?"

"Listen," she says. "I don't necessarily agree with all of your father's opinions, but I do see the need for you to learn life skills."

Instead of arguing with my mother, I turn the conversation toward her. "Is that what you took in school? Typing and home economics?"

The silence is brief but painful. "What else was I going to take? My parents were poor. I needed a job right after high school. If they offered bookkeeping, I'd have you take that, too."

I sigh. "But I don't want to work in an office. I want to be creative. Don't people get paid to draw those cartoons in the Sunday paper? They can't all work for free, can they? I mean, why else would they do it?"

"Maybe they have a second job," Lammie Pie reasons. She presses her lips together and turns down our street. Already the leaves are starting to turn to rust on the neighbor's tree, and the lawns are starting to yellow. The air has a sudden bite to it in the evenings and the fog lingers a little longer into the afternoon. "Listen. If you take typing and home economics this semester, I'll let you take drawing and painting next semester. Okay?"

I stare at her, disbelieving.

She pulls into the driveway and reaches underneath her seat. "Here." She hands me a small package. "It's your birthday present. I'm sorry it's late."

I rip through the gleaming blue wrapping paper. It's a dark-green leather-bound book. I flip through the pages. They are lined like college-ruled paper. On the side of the book, opposite its bound spine, is a golden lock. A key dangles from a chain.

"It's a diary, but you don't have to use it for that," Lammie Pie explains. "I thought you might want to write down the stories you tell your sisters so you can share them with your children someday."

I finger the golden lock and key.

"That's so your father won't see what you write," she explains. "You're almost a teenager. You need your privacy."

I gape at my mother. A seedling of understanding buds between us.

The next day, Cynthia convinces me to go shopping with her. "We need to get rid of the nerd look," she says. "Get you something fashionable."

I tug my ratty sweater over my breasts and narrow my eyes. "Is this Dad's idea?" I ask, suspiciously.

"No," she says, matter-of-factly, "it's Mom's idea. She's embarrassed you look like an old lady when you're not even a teenager yet."

I glance down at my baggy homemade pants that used to be snug around the waist and wonder if I look as terribly unfashionable as my sister says I do.

In the afternoon, Lammie Pie drops us off at the Eastridge Shopping Center. Cynthia and I wander through air-conditioned shops touching rough cotton and cotton blends, soft rayon and polyester, slippery satin and silk. Soft pastels and flashy bright solids tantalize me. I glimpse a teenage girl in a white T-shirt and jeans strutting in front of the full-length mirror and think of Antoinette. Suddenly, the baggy sweats I usually wear to hide my body make me feel more self-conscious than my curves.

"Want to try this?" Cynthia asks.

I glance at the shapeless top and wince. For the first time in my life, I rummage through the racks and select something form-fitting. "How about this?"

Cynthia raises her eyebrows at the white crop top. "Are you sure?" she asks.

I nod. I want to be like Antoinette with her Guess T-shirt and Jordache jeans, possessing style and sophistication.

In the dressing room, we try on jeans and T-shirts, miniskirts and tube tops. Cynthia tugs a body-hugging crop top over my head and smiles. "I can't believe you picked this out," she says. "This is one hand-me-down I'd take right now."

I turn around and gape in the mirror. My breasts swell against the fabric. The skin between my chest and belly is exposed. My legs stretch forever beneath the tiny skirt. When I turn around to see myself from all angles, my arms and legs swing awkwardly from their joints like doors opening from backward hinges. I almost trip over Cynthia, who giggles with delight.

"It's not funny," I snap, feeling like a stranger in my own body.

"You look fine," she says. "You just don't know how to move."

"No kidding." I examine myself again. These are the same clothes Antoinette wears, but they don't look the same on me. While Antoinette looks like a supermodel, I look like a floppy rag doll dressed for a nightclub. My shoulders slump with disappointment. *I'm never going to fit in*, I think. *I'll always look different even when I try to look the same.* Tears well up in my eyes, but I don't let them fall. *Maybe all it takes is practice with posture*, I think. I take a deep breath and imagine I am one of those girls in the magazine. With one step forward, I twirl around to see my transformation. But instead of turning like a ballerina, I trip over my own feet and stumble against the dressing room wall. Cynthia laughs.

Regaining my balance, I perch on the small dressing room seat and sigh. I will never be Antoinette. She has a life so far removed from my own that I can't even begin to imagine how to pretend to be like her. Disappointed with myself, I tug the shirt over my head and crumple it into a ball and toss it against the wall. "I don't want these clothes. They make me look like a slut!"

Cynthia taps her chin with a finger. "Not a slut," she says. "But not a virgin either."

"What's the difference?"

"It's not just the clothes. It's how you wear them. You need to learn how to walk and sit and stand like a slut if you want to look like a slut. You need a certain confidence you lack. But I can teach you it, if you'd like."

"No, thanks." Before I start to cry, I shove the clothes in a pile and slip back into my baggy sweat top and pants and bolt out of the dressing room. Anger pulses through my body, lighting up my steps. My hips may not sway like a tantalizing plaything, but they don't stand still like a plastic Barbie doll either. I don't calm down so I can do the right thing and find a style that suits me. Instead, I dwell on the fact that I will never be as cool as Antoinette or as brash as my sister.

"Wait!" Cynthia grabs the clothes and hustles after me. "We're getting these!"

"Why?" I ask, spinning around. My face burns with humiliation. *So I can look like a failure trying to fit in?* I think. Instead of telling her the truth, I make up a false reason. "So boys can pay more attention to me than to the teacher?"

"What's wrong with that?"

Quick, think of something. "I'm going to school to learn, not to star in a fashion show like you do."

Cynthia frowns. "You don't know how hard it is being your sister!" she shouts. "You're a nerd. I'm not. Teachers assume I'm smart and responsible. I have to teach everyone I'm beautiful and talented, too. It doesn't help my reputation when you keep dressing in clothes Mom made you or you sewed yourself. Even Mom and

Dad talk about how geeky you look. I'm embarrassed to be seen with you. I'm ashamed to call you my sister."

I grab the hangers from Cynthia and slam them on the counter. I want to fit in, but I don't know how. Maybe, just maybe, Cynthia can show me how and I'll learn. I'm a great student at school, why can't I be a great student at life? "Okay, but only if you show me how to wear them."

"Fine," Cynthia says. "Just don't take them off once you're at school like you do with the makeup."

"How do you know about that?"

"I have my sources." Her eyes narrow. I keep forgetting most of her friends have sisters and brothers my age. I wonder how she gets them to check up on me. Most of the time, I hang out alone, sulking in a corner, eating my salami and cheese sandwiches and completing as much homework as I can get done during breaks and lunch. I didn't think anyone noticed me. I don't dress to be noticed.

"Don't you want someone to love you?" Cynthia asks, grabbing the bag of paid for clothes.

I shrug. *I want to be comfortable with my body like Antoinette.* "If I do, I want to be loved for who I am, not how I look."

"Boys aren't like girls. They don't care what's inside. They only care about how you're packaged."

I grab the bag from her and pout. "Well, if I dress the way you and Dad and Mom want me to dress, I guess I'll have no problem."

Cynthia shakes her head. "If only there was a book that could teach you how to be graceful, then I wouldn't be so ashamed of being your sister."

"Maybe you should write one," I suggest.

Her eyes widen. "I'm kidding. Grace can't be taught from a book. It's something you feel in your bones." She slows her pace and turns to me. "See that girl over there? The one in the sleeveless dress?"

I glance over at the girl. She is standing by the escalator giggling with her girlfriends. A teenage boy saunters by, and she flashes him a coquettish smile.

"See how she barely tilts her head? How she shifts from foot to foot so slightly you can barely notice the swing in her hips?"

I nod.

"*That's* style." Cynthia picks up her pace, as if she is pretending she's not really with me although we are walking side by side. Without looking at me, she says, "You may be book smart, but you're street stupid."

I laugh. "You're right," I say, wrapping my arm around her waist and pulling her close. "And what's wrong with that?"

She bats me away. "Everything!"

————

Sierramont Middle School hasn't changed over the summer. But it seems like everyone else has.

The boys who competed with me last year in sixth grade ignore me now that we are in seventh grade. They stay on their side of the classroom and do not look at me. When I try to talk to them, they make excuses to leave. I am lonely until Kelly, a Mexican girl with glossy black hair and a face like a frog, invites me to have lunch with her. It is nice to belong, especially since the boys I used to hang out with no longer speak to me.

"Why do they act like they're afraid of me?" I ask Kelly.

She flips her black hair and smiles. "Boys are strange. Don't try to figure them out."

Rhoda, Kelly's friend since elementary school, agrees. "I have an older brother and he makes absolutely no sense to me whatsoever."

"But these guys used to be my best friends. We did everything together."

"Everything?" Kelly asks, raising her eyebrows.

I take a deep breath and watch two boys I've known since kindergarten walk across campus with their books tucked beneath their arms. As soon as I wave, they duck their heads and start to jog away. I frown. "We worked in the cafeteria. We worked on science projects. We beat each other up on the playground. We—"

"You beat each other up?" Rhoda asks.

"Yeah," I nod, like it is the most natural thing. "Just for fun."

"I didn't know getting beat up was fun," Rhoda says.

"It wasn't that bad. No one really got hurt."

"That's good." But from the tone of her voice I know she doesn't believe me.

"Why are you wearing makeup this year?" Kelly asks.

"I met a girl over the summer who looked absolutely fabulous in it."

"Don't your parents mind?" Rhoda asks.

I shake my head. "My father buys the makeup."

"Really?"

Suddenly, Kelly and Rhoda like my father, although they've never met him.

"I wish my dad would let me wear makeup," Kelly says. "As it is, I have to sneak money from my mom's purse and buy it on the sly."

"I wear my sister's makeup."

"I used to like the natural look," I say. "But sometimes cosmetics can enhance what you already have."

"And it makes guys go gaga," Kelly says, flipping her long black mane and fluttering her eyelashes. "I want them to find me beautiful."

Rhoda twirls a silver cross at the base of her neck. "I want a boyfriend. I don't want to study all the time. I want to have fun, too."

"What's fun about having a boyfriend?" I ask. Around campus, couples hold hands and sit close to each other on benches, touching and kissing. They gaze at each other with glossy eyes and stupid smiles, and forget to turn in their homework and study for tests. From what I can see, there is nothing glamorous about having a boyfriend. Unless you want to go to the school dances. Then you don't have to wait for someone to ask you to dance or feel silly trying to start up a conversation with someone who doesn't want to talk to you.

Kelly and Rhoda, however, see the situation differently. They clasp their hands over their hearts and toss back their heads and sigh. "We want to be in love."

They remind me of the women in the soap operas who pine for men they either cannot have or shouldn't have. I think they're both being ridiculous. "School's more important," I tell them. "When I grow up, I'm going to college and having a career before I even start dating."

Kelly snickers. "You're going to be an old maid."

"I am not!"

"Old maid," Rhoda echoes.

I endure the teasing. There is no way for me to remain friends with boys who pretend I don't exist. If Kelly and Rhoda are around, I join them. If they can't be found, I sit in the quad alone. After a while, I stop feeling lonely. I have books to read and homework to do.

A month later, Lammie Pie picks me up from school. She sees me saunter across the blacktop with my backpack slung over one shoulder, my feet clip-clopping with black ankle boots. My legs are bare up to the denim miniskirt. My breasts sway against the clingy white tank top. Even the knots in my curls have been smoothed down with mousse. I haul my books into the van and slide in next to her. When I shut the door, she leans over and says, "You look older than you are."

"Thanks," I say, although I am still getting used to my new look.

Lammie Pie drives. When we are out of the parking lot, she says, "I think you're getting too thin. Just look at those cheekbones. You look like a skeleton."

"It's the braces," I say. "I can't eat anything when the orthodontist tightens them."

It's true. Before school started, Chee took me to the orthodontist and had him place the silver discs and bands on my teeth. "She'll have to wear them for a couple of years," the orthodontist said, "but her smile will be worth the $10,000."

I swallow and glance out the van's window. Students cross the street like herded cattle. My mother brakes and turns on the stereo.

"I have algebra homework," I tell her. "Do you want to help me?"

"Fine, but you'll have to find someone else to tutor you when you get to trigonometry. I never got past geometry."

"Why don't you take trigonometry now?" I ask.

"I've forgotten everything," she says.

"Well, if you're like me, it won't take you long to remember."

She puckers her lips and steers. She is quiet for a while, turning the possibility over in her head. "What will your father say?"

"Who cares what he says? You're a grown-up, right?"

Lammie Pie gives me a quizzical look like I'm speaking a foreign language.

I explain. "When we were at the beauty salon in the mall, the woman who permed my hair said I had to obey my parents as long as I was a minor, but once I was grown up, I could do whatever I want."

"I wish it was that easy," Lammie Pie sighs. "When you're single, you may think you can conquer the world, but then you realize you don't have the money or the experience, and so your plans are put on hold until you do. When you're married, it gets even more complicated. Now you have to think about how your decisions will affect another person. And once you have children, you have to take into account their best interests, too."

I ponder her words, turning them over like stones. "So, if you wanted to go to college now, how would that affect us?"

Lammie Pie sighs again. "I don't want to go to college right now."

"Then what do you want to do?" I ask.

She glances at me and smiles. "I want to be your mommy. You're a part of me and so are your sisters. I don't want college courses to distract from that. That's why I work only part-time. I want to be home when you get out of school. I want to help you and your sisters with homework. I want to take Cynthia to dance lessons and volunteer to sew costumes. That's what I want more than anything in the whole world."

"Is that why you came back?" I ask. "To be with us?"

She parks the van and turns to me, taking my hands in her hands. We stare at each other. It is so quiet I can hear my heart thudding in my chest. "It's not the only reason," she says, squeezing my hands. "But it's the one that matters most of all."

13: UNEXPECTED

On Sunday, Lammie Pie hums as she cleans house, fluffing pillows and dusting. She tries to keep us quiet while Chee takes his afternoon nap before work. As two thirty rolls around, she notices Chee has not appeared in the kitchen to pack his lunch. She leaves the laundry in the hamper and stalks down the hall to rap on the bedroom door. When no one answers, she steps inside. Moments later, she rushes down the hall, screaming, "Angela! Cynthia! Elizabeth! Emergency!"

We gather in the living room. Elizabeth turns off the TV and sits on the floor. Cynthia shudders. I stand, afraid to move, wondering what is wrong.

"Your dad passed out on the toilet," she says. "I woke him up and got him into bed and called his doctor, who thinks it's another ulcer. The doctor wanted to send an ambulance, but I think I can get to the hospital quicker. Grandpa is coming to pick you up and take you to his house. I'll be back to pick you up once I know your father is okay."

We nod, grasping hands, silently praying.

Lammie Pie drapes Chee's arm around her shoulders. He leans against her and shuffles. Cynthia grabs his other arm and wraps it around her shoulder. I've never seen him so ashen and weak, as helpless as a baby.

After Lammie Pie leaves with Chee for the hospital, Cynthia races to her room, tears streaming down her face.

"What's wrong with her?" I ask Elizabeth.

"She's scared. Aren't you scared?"

I check my stomach, which always signals my resistance to change with a nasty gnarling hunger, but I am fine. For some reason, I am not worried. I know Chee will come back. Every year or two, he goes into the hospital to be treated for an ulcer and every time he returns with a prescription and a list of foods to avoid. He follows his doctor's orders for a while, but then lapses into his old habits, eating spicy, greasy foods and letting his anger and frustration build until the acids burn another hole through his stomach lining.

I go into the family room and knock on Cynthia's invisible door.

"Go away," she mumbles.

"What's wrong?" I ask. "Why are you crying?"

"Leave me alone!"

"Why are you so upset? I thought you hated Dad."

She turns to me, her red eyes glowing. "I never said I hated him!"

"You act like you do. You never listen to anything he says or do anything he asks."

"That doesn't mean I hate him. It means I just disagree with the way he's raising us, that's all. I still love him."

"You do?"

"Of course, I do, stupid! For a straight-A student, you sure don't have any common sense."

The doorbell rings. Elizabeth answers it. I hear Grandpa chuckle.

"Heh-heh-heh," he says, poking Elizabeth in the tummy. "Guess what I brought for you and your sisters?"

I walk across the living room and smile at Grandpa in his soft gray hat, green button-down shirt, gray slacks, and black steel-tipped shoes. He is shaped like a pear, small on top and round toward the bottom, a comforting shape, especially when he pulls you close for a hug. When he chuckles, his hazel eyes sparkle and his thin lips arch into a smile.

"Your daddy'll be all right," he says, holding out a candy bar. "Your mama's taking care of him. She's good at taking care of people, just like her mama."

Elizabeth takes the red-and-silver candy package and holds it carefully.

"You can eat it now." He winks. "You don't have to wait till after dinner like your daddy says."

Grandpa glances up at me, and his face becomes grave for a moment. "Don't study too much. You don't want to end up like your daddy."

"I won't," I say.

"Promise?"

I nod.

He hands me a candy bar.

"Where's Cindy?"

No one calls any of us by nicknames, but somehow Grandpa can call us whatever he likes.

"She's in her room crying," Elizabeth whispers.

Grandpa waddles into the family room and squeezes into the doorway of Cynthia's makeshift room. He waves a candy bar at her and smiles. "Coming or going?" he asks.

She grabs the candy bar and gives him a hug.

"Like I was telling your sisters, your daddy's going to be okay," Grandpa says. "Your mama takes good care of him, just like she takes good care of you."

"But she's not a doctor," Cynthia sniffs. "She can't stop the bleeding."

"No, but God can." Although Grandpa stopped going to church after hearing nothing but sermons on tithing, he maintains a deep faith in God and an everlasting belief in miracles. "Look at you girls," he says, opening the door of his Datsun. "The doctors said your mama couldn't have children. And God blessed her with you three. The best girls in the world!"

We sit in the backseat of the stuffy Datsun with the hot black vinyl sticking to our thighs. We eat our candy bars in silence. The chocolate smears on our fingers and the wafers dissolve on our tongues.

Grandpa and Grandma live on the eastside of San Jose in the same house Lammie Pie moved into when she was fourteen. Grandpa pulls up into the driveway and parks the Datsun. The house is the same lime green with white trim as it has always been. The screen door slaps open and our cousins, nine-year-old Bobby and four-year-old Becky, tumble out onto the green oasis of lawn stretching from the porch to the sidewalk. Cynthia, Elizabeth, and I crawl out of the backseat and chase after them. No matter what happens to our father, we are relieved to have a day of play for ourselves.

———

By the time the sun disappears behind the roof and a brisk wind whips hair across our faces, Grandpa steps outside and calls us in for dinner. We sit at the rectangular table beside the sliding glass door leading to the backyard where Grandpa's plum and cherry trees drop their luscious fruit. Although the sky still cups a drop of amber-gray light, inside it is too dark to eat without Grandma flicking on the overhead light.

We hunch over our plates of meatloaf, mashed potatoes, and green beans with our dirty faces and grubby weekend clothes much like the subjects in van Gogh's painting, *The Potato Eaters*. I have been studying his paintings in a book I checked out of the library, dreaming of next semester when I will finally get to explore art with color.

We are halfway through dinner when the doorbell rings. Grandpa waddles to the door to answer it.

Our mother's voice is soft and familiar.

Grandma rises from the table. She looks like a question mark with her hunched back and pencil-thin legs. Her floral house dress fits like a potato sack and her white knee-length socks are stuffed into black shoes. She shuffles across the linoleum. Lammie Pie greets her at the edge of the kitchen's dining area.

Before glancing up at Lammie Pie's wan face, Grandma asks, "How's Dave?" Her hoarse voice usually has a rough edge to it like she's always angry or upset about someone or something, but when she asks about our father, her crabby voice lowers into a scratchy whisper bordering on tears.

Grandma loves our father. She used to make a special trip to the grocery store every Sunday after church to buy a gallon of milk whether or not they needed it. Even when the express lane opened or other checkers waved to her to come into their line, Grandma refused to move. "I want to listen to that funny Chinaman," she said. Eventually, Grandma insisted her daughters come and meet the Chinese checker. Mary Anne didn't care too much for his jokes. Mildred didn't like the way spittle flew from his mouth when he stuttered. Only Lammie Pie seemed as enchanted with him as Grandma was. Months later, when Dave finally asked for Lammie Pie's phone number, Grandma smiled and said, "I hope he asks you out and I hope you say yes." Months after they started dating, Grandma smiled and said, "I hope he asks you to marry him and I hope you say yes."

Lammie Pie looks down at her mother. Her voice trembles. "They're going to operate."

"When?" Grandpa asks.

"Right now."

"Why aren't you there?" Grandma demands. "I've got the kids' dinner. Go and be with him. He needs you."

"I can't go into the operating room with him," Lammie Pie explains. "He's in good hands. The girls need me more." Her voice catches as she glances at Cynthia sitting at the table. "And I need them."

Grandma scoots another chair to the already-overcrowded table. "If you aren't going back to the hospital, you might as well stay for dinner. I made extra."

"No, thanks," Lammie Pie says. "I'm tired. I think I'll take the kids home."

We say good-bye to Bobby and Becky and hug and kiss Grandpa and Grandma good-bye. In the van, Lammie Pie turns up the stereo to listen to a happy song. After a while, tears sprinkle her cheeks and her hands shake against the steering wheel.

"Are you all right?" I ask.

She nods, wiping away her tears.

"Are you scared about Dad?" I ask.

She nods again, wiping away more tears.

Cynthia reaches from behind and cups her hand on Lammie Pie's shoulder. "I'm scared, too," she says.

"Me, too," whispers Elizabeth.

I feel strangely removed from everyone's concern for Chee. Over the last twelve years, I have seen my father ill, but he has always recovered. I can't imagine why the doctors are going to operate. I glance around the van at my family. Lammie Pie grabs a tissue from the dash to wipe her tears. Cynthia leans against the back of Lammie Pie's seat with her hand firmly on Lammie Pie's shoulder. Her grave face seems as ghostly as a full moon on Halloween night. Elizabeth curls up in her seat with her knees drawn up to her chest. Her brown eyes glitter with tears. I sit back and wonder if I should be scared, too.

14: Say a Prayer

My father is still in the hospital two days after the operation. I can't concentrate at school. In the stale, air-conditioned rooms, I pretend to be the perfect student. I sit through algebra and practice writing formulas until the formulas don't mean anything any longer. In history, I write down significant dates and forget them as quickly as I write them down. In language arts, I read the same paragraph five times. It still doesn't make sense. No one knows anything is wrong. During lunch, I pass Kelly and Rhoda sitting beneath a shady tree with their new boyfriends. They are too busy snuggling and giggling to wave hello.

When school is over, I stroll toward the yellow curb and pace back and forth, scanning the parking lot. Grandpa pulls up in his gray-green Datsun and honks. I slide across the black vinyl seat and ask if there is any news.

"Don't know," Grandpa says. "Your mama's visiting him."

My sisters and I spend the afternoon inside of the green-and-white house. A standing fan in the hallway blows hot air back and forth. Grandpa sinks into his rocking chair and lights a pipe of sweet tobacco. Grandma irons while watching her soaps. My sisters and I sit on the couch and finish our homework.

Lammie Pie picks us up after dinner. She looks pale and exhausted. She hasn't slept in days. She doesn't talk about our father on the drive. At home, she helps us get ready for bed. After we bathe and brush our teeth and comb our hair, Lammie Pie gathers us into the living room. She asks us to kneel with her.

"Why?" Elizabeth asks.

"We're going to say a prayer for Daddy. So he gets better soon."

"Should we pray to Virgin Mary?" Cynthia asks.

"We're going to pray to St. Jude."

"Who's he?" I ask.

"The patron saint of lost causes."

Cynthia screams. "Why didn't you tell us Dad's going to die?"

"He's not," Lammie Pie says, trying to reassure her. "It just means we need a miracle."

"He's going to die!" Cynthia stands up and runs to her room behind the Chinese screen painted with the two cranes that symbolize long life.

Lammie Pie makes the sign of the cross and begins to pray, "Dear St. Jude . . ."

Elizabeth and I bow our heads and listen to Lammie Pie's prayer. We wait until the end when we whisper, "Amen," and cross ourselves. Lammie Pie gathers us into her arms for a big hug. "Go to your room and wait for me to tuck you in. I'm going to talk to your sister for a few minutes, first."

Elizabeth and I stand up and walk to the edge of the hallway. When Lammie Pie disappears behind Cynthia's screen, Elizabeth and I quietly return to the sofa. We want to listen.

In the other room, we hear Cynthia shout, "I don't believe in God. I don't believe in things I can't see or touch."

Elizabeth and I glance at each other.

Lammie Pie's voice is clear and modulated. "Of course, you believe in God. If you didn't, you wouldn't be here."

"Liar!"

"When I was first married, the doctors said I was infertile. I had cysts surgically removed from my fallopian tubes. I took six different fertility drugs. It took four whole years before I conceived Angela."

"I know," Cynthia sobs. "I've heard the story a million times from Dad. Especially how he promised God and the Virgin Mary that he'd be the best father in the whole world."

"Well, he is, isn't he?" Lammie Pie demands. "How many of your friends' fathers are involved in their lives? Your dad is with you every morning. He teaches you things before you learn them in school."

"I wish he wasn't so involved," Cynthia says. "I wish he'd leave us alone." Her voice rises to a dangerous pitch. "He's always picking on me to clean up my room, to be an A student, to listen and obey, to be perfect. Why doesn't he take the log out of his own eye, first? Why doesn't he stop flirting with other women? Why doesn't he stop gambling? Why doesn't he stop shoplifting? Why doesn't he stop begging for money from his brothers? Why doesn't he stop bossing everyone else around and take control over his own life? Isn't that why he's sick?"

Elizabeth and I glance at each other in silent terror. She squeezes my hand for reassurance; I squeeze it back for comfort.

Lammie Pie's voice is calm and measured. "Your father tries very hard," she says. "He's not perfect."

"Then why does he expect us to be?"

After a long pause, she whispers, "I don't know."

Elizabeth and I scramble to our feet, but it's too late. Lammie Pie sees us sitting on the sofa, eavesdropping. "I thought I told you both to go to bed and wait for me."

Elizabeth and I bolt down the hall.

After tucking Elizabeth in, Lammie Pie peeks inside my room. My heartbeat thunders in my chest. I think she is going to yell at me, but her voice is soft and warm. "Want to stay up a little bit longer?" she asks.

A wave of excitement flows over me. I throw the sheets off my body and shove my feet into slippers. I don't know or care why my mother has chosen to spend time with me. I'm just happy my mother wants to be my friend.

In the kitchen, Lammie Pie goes to the stove to brew a cup of tea. I sit down at the table and wait. Watching Lammie Pie's deliberate movements, a different thought strikes me, one that makes me incredibly sad. Maybe my mother wants to tell me the truth: Chee is dying and there is nothing the doctors can do for him. My hands tremble with panic. I can't imagine life without my father, no matter how hard I try. I consider leaving the table to avoid knowing more than I want to know, but on her way to the pantry, Lammie Pie touches my hand. My body suffuses with her tenderness. I decide to stay and hear the news, good or bad.

From a hidden spot in the pantry, Lammie Pie finds a box of Danish cookies Chee was saving for a Christmas gift and peels back the plastic seal. Every year, Chee saves half the gifts we receive and recycles them as gifts during the upcoming year. "You never know when you might need a gift," Chee reasons. "Just in case someone surprises us with an unexpected gift, we don't need to send him away empty-handed." If Cynthia is right and Chee dies, he will not be around to yell at Lammie Pie for eating this "just in case" gift.

"Want one?" Lammie Pie asks.

The butter cookies gleam with sugar sparkles. My stomach rumbles with hunger, but I shake my head.

"Sure?"

The sugar sparkles wink promises of happiness. I take one shaped as a pretzel. Its hard texture breaks into brittle flakes in my mouth and wedges between the wires of my braces. I glance around for a glass of milk. Lammie Pie seems to read my mind and walks over to the dishwasher removing a clean cup and filling it with fresh milk.

"Thanks," I say.

Lammie Pie finishes her second cookie. She brushes the crumbs from her hands and sips her tea. "You know, Cynthia is right," she says. "Your father is sick because he worries too much about what other people think. He doesn't live for himself. He's still trying to please his mother." Lammie Pie hunches over her tea and sighs. "When I called the hospital at work, I was told he had been released from ICU to a regular room. But when I got there this afternoon, he was back in ICU."

"Why? What happened?"

"Uncle George and Aunt Lil brought Mah-Mah down to see him. She started talking to him about how he needs to have a boy in order for her to leave any money to him after she dies. She said she loves him more than John and Bill and Jimmy combined. She said she wants to leave him everything, but she can't because he doesn't have a son.

"So he got upset. He started yelling at her in Cantonese. The nurses asked her to leave. But it was too late. The damage was already done. His blood pressure rose. And the bleeding started again. By the time I came to visit him, he was back in ICU." Lammie Pie selects another cookie. She nibbles the edges with her front teeth. "He was conscious when I got there. For a while, I was afraid he might not be. He had his eyes closed."

"What did he say?"

"Nothing at first. He let me do the talking for a change." A half smile flickers across her face. "I asked what happened and he told me. I got angry and did something I don't do enough of. I told him exactly what I thought and felt. I told him to grow up; he doesn't live with the woman anymore, who cares if he doesn't have boys, and at least his girls are healthy and smart, what else could he want? But he wasn't happy. I could tell by the way he pursed his lips. Then I told him the rest of the truth, the stuff I knew would hurt more than anything I've ever said before. I told him Mah-Mah is going to kill him if he lets her. And then who will she leave her money to? Bill's kids and Jimmy's kids and maybe Lil's kids. But it still won't go to him. Why die for something he'll never have anyway?"

"What did he say?"

"Nothing."

"What did you do?"

"I left."

Her blue eyes glitter. I want to comfort her like I comfort my sisters. Slowly, I reach across the table and touch the back of her blue-veined hand. Her skin looks cool and smooth like a porcelain doll, but it is coarse and dry like parchment paper.

Just when I feel close to my mother, she pulls her hand away and says, "I probably shouldn't be telling you this. You're too young, I know, but I need to talk to someone."

I am hurt and offended. After everything I have been through this past summer, I don't feel too young for my mother's confidences. I think I can handle whatever Lammie Pie wants to say, even if I don't understand it all. But I don't tell my mother any of this. Instead, I ask, "What about Joanne?"

Lammie Pie sniffs and rubs the tip of her nose. "Joanne quit work. I haven't spoken to her since."

"When did she quit?" I ask, feeling strange because I know so little about my mother's life.

"After Mr. Buckley's party."

"Why?"

"She said she needed a better-paying job. So she went to work for the county as a clerk."

Again I am stung with hurt. How can I be a friend to my mother when I know next to nothing about her life? My voice is crisp, almost brittle, when I stammer, "Why didn't you tell us?"

Lammie Pie shrugs. "Why would you care anyway? No one wants me to have friends."

"Only Dad says that. Cynthia, Elizabeth, and I want to have friends just as badly as you do." There is an edge of anger in my voice. I don't understand why she pits me against her. Doesn't she know I'm not my father?

Lammie Pie grabs a tissue and dabs her eyes. "Every night I listened to Cynthia tell me how awful the girls treated her at school because she didn't fit in. She's too bright and she's too pretty and she's too talented and she's too fashionable. I told her to start her own group, don't bother trying to fit in with people who don't want her anyway. So she did. And now she has more friends than anyone else."

"Why don't you follow your own advice?"

Lammie Pie shrugs. "I guess I'm too old."

"No, you're not."

She stares at the orange wall, at the painting of Jesus and the twelve disciples at the Last Supper, at the crucifix hanging above the doorway. "You're right. I've tried. You don't know how hard I've tried. But your father won't let anyone visit. If I want to have friends, I'm forced to live two very different lives: one at work and one at home. And after a while, it becomes absolutely exhausting. Almost as exhausting as taking care of everything while your father's in the hospital." Her voice crumbles into a sob. "I'm sorry," she says. "I shouldn't be breaking down in front of you like this. It isn't the right thing to do."

"What is the right thing?"

"To be strong."

I stare at my mother, the woman who lost thirty pounds in thirty days, the woman who ran away because she felt her husband wanted to control her, but came back when she realized she couldn't live without her daughters, and I wonder who could be stronger.

She straightens her spine and dabs her eyes with a tissue. "I've kept you up past your bedtime. You should go to sleep. Don't you have a test tomorrow?"

I nod, knowing that isn't the real reason why she wants me to go to bed.

She takes her cup of tea into the living room and turns on the TV. Setting her cup on the coffee table, she gets out her cutting board from the closet and unfolds it on the carpet. Kneeling with needles in her mouth, she arranges a flimsy pattern on scarlet linen. I lean against the doorjamb and watch her for a few moments longer. She may not be able to stitch up my father and make him better, but she can sew a new dress for my sisters or me. I know how to sew, but it doesn't release the pent-up feelings inside of me like it does for my mother. Not even drawing can do that for me anymore.

I turn and go down the hall to my bedroom. After lying awake for a half hour, I decide to get out the blank book my mother bought for my birthday. With a ballpoint pen and a flashlight, I begin to write.

15: EDUCATION

The next day at school, my language arts teacher, Mrs. McNiff, decides to teach class outside. "Tired of all that recycled air," she says, sitting with her back against the trunk of a tree. Her black hair flaps across her face in the warm breeze. Stippled shadows dance over the papers resting in her lap beneath her hands. I shift on the grass and rub my dripping nose. We have just settled on the newly mown lawn and already my head throbs and my eyes water and my nose runs. But I don't ask to be excused. I want to know what grade I got on last week's assignment.

"Instead of reading from our books, I thought I'd read to you some of my favorite stories," she says. Flipping through the pages in her lap, she brings one to the forefront and starts to read. "When I was nine, my teacher took me on a hot air balloon ride. . . ."

I hold my breath. I can't believe it. She's reading my story!

Half-listening, I glance at the other students to gauge their responses just as I do when I am telling my sisters a story. Some of the boys lean forward and stop pulling up grass. A few of the girls lean back on their elbows and cross their ankles. The rest of the class doodles in their notebooks or stares at the sky. When Mrs. McNiff is finished with the story, some of the students applaud.

"Guess who wrote that?" she asks.

"Jimmy," someone says.

Mrs. McNiff shakes her head. "Maybe I shouldn't embarrass her."

"Her?" Denise asks. "It sounds like an adventure a boy would write about."

My shoulders tense. I hope no one guesses and I hope Mrs. McNiff doesn't reveal who the writer is.

"Give up?" She flicks through the papers and begins to read another story.

"I thought you were going to tell us who wrote it."

Mrs. McNiff glances up and frowns. "I changed my mind." She continues reading about a tourist lost in Italy. I sit mesmerized by the timber of her voice, the cadence of the words. I listen for a continual flow of movement and wince when the narrator jumps from a gondola and ends up in a church. In my mind, I bridge the gap with a transition, navigating the narrator from the waterways through the marketplace to the crumbling steps of the church. By the time Mrs. McNiff is finished, I've rewritten a quarter of the story, including the ending. The next essay Mrs. McNiff reads is more coherent. I grow frustrated trying to find fault with it. The essay draws me deeper and deeper into the everyday events of the narrator who ends up in a terrible auto accident by the time the essay has ended. When Mrs. McNiff stops reading, I raise my hand.

"Who wrote that?" I ask.

"I'm not revealing any of the writers," Mrs. McNiff says. "You'll just have to be content with listening for today."

"But I want to know."

She smiles sweetly at me and selects the final essay. I forget to listen. My gaze darts from each face, hoping to decipher the mystery writer. My palms itch. I try to imagine who has been in an auto accident, but I can't tell from looking at the students. Maybe Kelly might know. I nudge her shoulder. "Do you know who wrote the story about the accident?"

She shrugs. "Why? Did it upset you?"

"No, I was just curious, that's all."

The bell rings. After the students have dispersed, I linger beside Mrs. McNiff who continues sitting beneath the tree. I kneel down in front of her. "Can you tell me who wrote the story about the accident?"

She smiles slyly. "Are you jealous?"

"No," I say, too quickly. "I just want to know, that's all."

Mrs. McNiff licks her bottom lip and rifles through the essays. I glance down, hoping to catch the author's name printed on top of the page, but it is my essay she hands to me. "I always look forward to reading your assignments. I never know what's going to happen next. Don't worry about the stories other people write about. Continue writing the stories only you can tell."

I sigh. "Why won't you tell me?"

"When I saw the expression on your face when I started reading your essay, I knew you'd never forgive me for embarrassing you. So I changed my mind and decided to keep everyone's anonymity, all right?"

I nod, but I'm not satisfied. "I promise I won't tell."

She shoves the remaining essays into her black bag and stands up to leave. "You should get going to your next class. Don't want to be tardy and end up with a referral."

Reluctantly, I turn and walk away. By the time I cross the threshold of algebra, the bell rings. I slip into my seat and glance down at my essay. On the top center of the first page, there is an A+ circled. I flush with pride. Wait till Chee sees it!

But Chee is still in intensive care.

"The doctors are going to release him next week," Lammie Pie tells us that night after dinner. "The doctors want to make sure he's stopped bleeding. If not, he may need to have his entire stomach removed."

"But how will he eat?" Elizabeth asks.

Lammie Pie rinses the dishes and loads them in the dishwasher. Her movements are as slow and precise as if she is being graded for the task. The phone rings. She gallops to answer it.

"Hello?"

My sisters and I pause from wiping the table, sweeping the floor, and packing our lunches for tomorrow. Our gazes focus on Lammie Pie's face, the creases around her lips, the lines around her eyes, the wrinkles on her brow.

"He's still in ICU," she explains to the caller. "I don't think they'll let you visit. Maybe you should come by next week. The doctors think he might be home then. Just don't bring Mah-Mah. I don't want her to upset him.

"He's sensitive around her," she explains. "I think that's why he got ill—because he can't please her—he's tried three times to get a son and each time he's gotten a daughter. No, I don't think we'll try one more time. Isn't three enough? Why don't you and Lil have kids?" She seals her lips. "I don't think she should visit. I'll call the hospital and tell them not to admit her. They have security, you know. I'm his wife. They'll honor my wishes."

She hangs up before the conversation can continue.

"Who was that?" Cynthia asks.

"Uncle John." Lammie Pie picks up a glass from the sink. She rinses it beneath the water and places it upside down on the top rack. "He wants to visit your father, but I told him I didn't think it was a good idea."

"What did he say when you asked him why he doesn't have kids?"

"I don't know. I wasn't listening."

"C'mon," Cynthia pleads. "Tell us."

Lammie Pie pours detergent and closes the door. She sets the dial to Normal. Water gushes through the pipes. She stands up and dries her hand on a dish towel. Her eyes are as blue and watery as the cornflowers Mr. Buckley sent to comfort Lammie Pie. "When your father invited his family to our wedding everyone except Uncle John showed up."

"What does that have to do with what he said?" Cynthia asks.

"He doesn't like us," Lammie Pie says. "He doesn't think we belong in the Lam family."

Cynthia scoffs. "He acts like he's the one who doesn't belong, not us."

"Is he coming to visit?" Elizabeth asks. "Because I don't want to have to share my room again."

"You haven't shared your room with anyone since Mah-Mah visited two years ago," Lammie Pie says. "That's why your sister is sleeping in the family room I had built because I wanted more space for me." She tosses the dish towel across the room. Elizabeth and I dodge the dish towel that hits the wall behind us. "Everything I've always wanted I had to sacrifice for someone," Lammie Pie sobs. "I couldn't go to college because my parents didn't make enough money. I couldn't get the job I wanted because I didn't have any experience. I couldn't have a baby without doctors getting involved. And when I finally had a baby, it wasn't a boy, it was a girl. I couldn't buy a two-story house with a spiral staircase because your dad doesn't make enough money. We had to borrow $10,000 from Mah-Mah to afford this place. And when we finally saved enough money to pay her back, we didn't have enough equity to move, so I begged to have the family room addition. All I want right now is for you kids to go to bed on time so I can take a bath!"

Lammie Pie stomps down the hall and slams the door to her bedroom.

Elizabeth starts to cry. "You made her mad at us." She picks up the dish towel and chases Cynthia. "You asked her what Uncle John said and you should've kept your mouth shut." She flicks the dish towel against Cynthia's back. Cynthia squeals and darts through the living room and disappears behind the Chinese folding screen.

"Leave her alone, Elizabeth!" I run after Elizabeth and grab the dish towel from her hands. "It's nobody's fault Mom is upset. Let's just get ready for bed. I'll tell you a story."

"A happy one?" Elizabeth asks.

"Yes." I stroke her soft hair.

Cynthia stands on her bed and peers over the screen. "Can I listen, too?"

"Of course," I say. "But you have to get ready for bed quickly, as I want to surprise Mom and have us all in bed before she gets out of her room, okay?"

My sisters scramble to the hall bathroom and jostle for room in front of the sink. The water runs in the sink long after they have filled their cups. "Don't waste water. Turn it off," I say, mimicking Chee. My sisters turn the faucet off and finish brushing their teeth.

The bedroom door opens. Lammie Pie glowers at me, then at my sisters.

"We're getting ready for bed," I explain. I want her to know I'm trying to erase her frustration, to eliminate as many of the things that bother her as I can. "Why don't you take a bath? When I'm done praying and telling a story, I'll scrub your back."

Her face softens against the electric light. "Would you?" she asks.

"Of course," I tell her. "Just let me get them to bed first."

After my sisters are tucked beneath the covers, I clean the tub for Lammie Pie's bath. I sprinkle Ajax cleaner on the dirty porcelain and wet a sponge. Using the attached hose on the faucet, I spray the tub clean with warm water.

I go into the kitchen and set the kettle on the stove. In the pantry I find a box of hot chocolate. I shake the tin of Danish cookies. Nothing rattles. I peel back the lid. It's empty.

The floorboards creak. I glance up at Lammie Pie. She flushes and snatches the empty tin from my hands.

Her face hardens. "Go to bed. I don't need my daughter judging me."

"Judging you?" My body bristles with anger over her false accusation. "I wasn't judging you." I stare at her, at the puckers of material clinging to her full hips and thighs. She's gained a few pounds since Chee's been in the hospital, but I hadn't noticed it until now. I slam the pantry door. "I'm not Dad. I don't care what you weigh." My voice cracks. I remember all the pictures I used to draw of her, and how I always wanted to have blue eyes like her. "You're beautiful," I say. "I've always thought you were beautiful." She stares at me in disbelief, and my chest aches from longing. How can I convince her that her beauty goes beyond the number of pounds that register on the scale? "Whenever people say I look like you, I feel beautiful."

She pouts, and for a moment, I'm not sure whether she's going to shout or cry. Her hands tremble, and she drops the empty tin on the linoleum. It clatters, and I bend down to pick it up. She mumbles, "I get so wound up trying to do everything that by the end of the day I'm just a bundle of nerves and I don't know what to do so I eat to calm down."

"You don't have to do everything," I say. "We're old enough to help."

Tears crest in her blue eyes. "None of you can make your father better."

I reach out to touch her, and she does not pull away. We embrace, and all the softness about her that I loved as a child is still there, but it's not as comforting.

"I'm so ashamed," she mumbles into my shoulder. "I want to be strong for you and your sisters, but I'm so weak."

"I think you're the best mom we could have," I tell her. "I wouldn't want anyone else."

"Your father wouldn't cry."

"He cried when you were gone."

"He did?" She pulls back and wipes her eyes with the back of her hand.

"We all did. We missed you. Just like we all miss Dad now."

She sniffs, considering my words. "Maybe I'll go ahead and take that bath. If you don't mind washing my back?"

I nod.

While she fills the tub, I empty a packet of hot chocolate into a cup and pour hot water till the cup is almost full. The phone rings. I wipe my hands on a dish towel and answer it on the third ring.

"Hello?" I ask, wondering who could be calling so late.

"Who is this?" the caller asks.

"It's Angela. Who is this?"

"Oh, the outspoken one," the man says. "It's Uncle John."

I haven't spoken to him since his red-egg party months ago. My instinct is to hang up, but my body won't move. It's like I've become a statue, frozen by the sound of his voice.

When I don't say anything, he asks, "Did your mom tell you to pick up the phone because she's afraid to talk to me?"

"She's not afraid of you. She's taking a bath. Maybe you should call back tomorrow."

A pregnant pause fills the space before he says, "Tell her I'm sorry. I didn't mean to upset her. I'll honor her wishes and not visit your father until he is released from the hospital." He pauses again. "How are you?" he asks.

No one has bothered to ask me how I'm doing and for a moment

I don't know how to respond. "I'm doing better." I swallow hard and twist the phone cord around my wrist. "At first it was a little difficult to concentrate at school because I was worried about my father, but I got an A+ on an essay."

"Congratulations! What did you write about?"

"Traveling in a hot air balloon."

"When did your parents take you?"

"They didn't. I had a teacher who flew hot air balloons as a hobby. She took me flying with her when I got the highest grade in the class."

"Impressive." He lowers his voice. "Listen, what I'm going to say to you is confidential. I know your father works hard, just as hard as Jimmy, Bill, and George do, but he's not a rich man. And I know you're not a boy, but that doesn't mean you don't deserve to go to college. I know you have the grades, and I have faith you'll keep them up through high school. But if you ever need help paying for tuition or books, just let me know. I'd like to help in any way I can, okay?"

"Why?"

Uncle John chuckles. "Did you forget already? I'm a new man." His voice bursts with pride. "I volunteer at the senior center and the humane society. I don't yell or curse anymore. I even take Aunt Lil with me everywhere I go. And it's all because of you."

"Me?" The surprise almost makes me lose my grip on the receiver.

"That's why I want to see your father. I know he's hard on you and your sisters, and he worries about everything. I want him to know how lucky he is to have you and your sisters."

"Maybe you should call him," I suggest.

"If they let me talk to him, I will."

Lammie Pie's voice floats down the hall. "I have to go," I say, remembering my promise to wash my mother's back.

"Okay, keep up the good work in school. And remember to tell your mother I'm sorry."

"I will. Goodnight." I feel light with relief as I hang up the phone.

As I kneel beside the tub and pick up a wet wash cloth and squeeze warm water down my mother's ivory back, I tell her Uncle John called.

"What did he want?" she snaps.

"He called to apologize. He says he's going to honor your wishes and wait till Dad gets home before he visits."

"Is that all?" she asks.

I remember my promise to keep Uncle John's desire to help me through college a secret, but I think I can trust my mother so I tell her. Everything.

"Aren't you lucky?" Lammie Pie says. "I wish I had a wealthy relative when I was young so I could have gone to college."

"You can still go back," I remind her. "I can watch my sisters while you're in school."

She shakes her head. "Not now. I've got too much going on already."

"Maybe later," I say, handing her a towel.

She steps out of the bath, her body glistening wet, and suddenly, the desire to capture her beauty on the page takes hold of me, and I want nothing more than a pencil and some paper.

16: HOMECOMING

I don't know if Uncle John spoke with my father. Lammie Pie won't tell me, and I don't bother to ask. I'm too busy with school and helping out at home.

In the evenings, after dinner, while Cynthia and Elizabeth watch TV and Lammie Pie visits Chee in the hospital, I draw. In my bedroom, at my desk, I sit with a blank sheet of typing paper. Strong sunlight floods through the window overlooking the backyard where Chee planted an orange tree for good luck. Over the last few months, I've discovered it takes a lot more than good luck to get through hard times. At first, I didn't have a word for it until one afternoon in language arts when Mrs. McNiff discussed a character in a short story who had endured several hardships. "He survived because he had resilience," she explained. "When times got tough, he bent like the trunk of a tree in a windstorm instead of snapping off like its branches. Sometimes along the coast where the wind is strong, you will see trees that grow in the direction of the wind. They have learned to adapt and have become stronger because of it. That's resilience." As I sit and sketch my mother's profile, from her high forehead to her small chin, I wonder whether or not I'll learn resilience.

Since Chee has been gone, I have noticed a couple of changes. I no longer lie awake listening for his flip-flops slapping down the hall. I no longer hide my art books or my artwork. I've taken the dolls off my shelves and replaced them with the art books I've checked out of the library. On my bulletin board, over the award certificates I've received for exemplary academic performance in all subjects, I pin my drawings of Cinderella, my mother, my sisters, and my Chow dog radio. I leave my diary on the nightstand with a pen, ready to write whenever inspiration strikes.

Every night when Lammie Pie returns from the hospital, we kneel down on the living room carpet, hold hands, and pray for Chee to get well. Even Cynthia bows her head and recites the memorized prayers. During the day, Lammie Pie wears the Immaculate Heart of Mary around her neck. She brings one with her to the hospital to pin on Chee's gown. Lammie Pie tells us Grandma walks to church each day and lights a candle, prays the rosary, and drops coins in the collection box, hoping Chee will get well soon. Every night Chee's sister, Aunt Lil, calls to inquire about his health. Lammie Pie makes her swear not to bring Mah-Mah if she decides to visit. Aunt Lil tells Lammie Pie she will wait for Chee to come home before she visits, but she will keep him in her family's prayers.

By the end of the following week, Chee is released from the hospital. On the day Lammie Pie brings him home, my sisters and I decide to surprise him by cleaning the entire house. Even Cynthia picks up her clothes, makes her bed, and dusts her furniture.

By the time we shove the vacuum cleaner into the hall closet, the garage door rattles up and the van rumbles into the garage.

"They're here," Elizabeth says.

Fear and anticipation race through my body. My heartbeat stutters in my chest. Sweat moistens my hands. I sit on the sofa next to Elizabeth and say, "I hope I didn't forget anything."

Cynthia shakes her head. "I don't know why you worry so much. He won't yell at you. You're his favorite. You never do anything wrong."

"That's not true," I say, thinking of all the times I've failed him.

The kitchen door creaks open, and Chee enters along with Lammie Pie. His knees buckle. Cynthia bolts up from the sofa and patters across the linoleum, wrapping her arms around his waist, trying to steady him. When he glances up, his dark eyes glow above his hollow cheekbones. My chest contracts with fear and sorrow. This is not my father; this is a man who has been gravely ill.

Chee holds Cynthia and asks, "Why you crying? I'm all right. No need to cry."

"I thought you were going to die," Cynthia says.

"Not die," Chee says. "Just operate."

"Let me get him into the living room," Lammie Pie says. "Then you guys can talk all night."

Chee shuffles into the living room and pats Elizabeth on the head. I stand up and offer him my hand to help him sit down on the sofa. He frowns and shakes his head.

"You help me up," he says. "I sit down all right." He plops down on the sofa and sighs.

Elizabeth tries to climb into his lap, but Lammie Pie shoos her away. "He has stitches," she warns. Elizabeth pouts for a moment before sitting back on the cushions and leaning her head against his arm. She tilts her head back and smiles. "We missed you," she says.

Cynthia brings him a glass of water and a handful of pills. "Mom says you need to take these." She hands them to him.

"Later."

Cynthia stands with her hands full, refusing to leave.

Chee takes the pills and gulps them down with water.

Lammie Pie turns toward the kitchen to make dinner.

As she leaves, I suddenly feel afraid, as if she is leaving me alone. I walk after her. "May I help you cook?"

She frowns. "Why don't you go talk to your father? He hasn't seen you in a couple of weeks."

She doesn't understand. I can't talk to him. I'm scared. When Chee was gone, I felt strong, stronger than I've felt in all my life, but now that he's back, I feel weak, much weaker than I've felt before he left for the hospital. Sure, I feel guilty for not welcoming him like my sisters, but the guilt does not eclipse the fear I have of being with him again. With my insecurities bobbing on the surface, I rush down the hall into my room and throw open my closet door, searching for the box of dolls. I want to place them back on the bookshelves before my father notices the difference.

By the time I drag the box into the center of my bedroom, my heart is thundering in my chest and my palms slip with sweat.

"What you doing?"

I glance up, startled to find Chee standing in the doorway, hovering like an apparition.

I try to swallow, but my throat is tight, too tight to speak. *Don't be scared*, I think. *Practice resilience.*

He glances around my room, absorbing the contents with a curious patience I have never known him to have. "What books are those?" he asks, pointing.

I breathe and find my voice. "Art books. I checked them out at the library. Mom said I can take painting next semester, and I want to get a head start, learn about the history, the different mediums, and the various techniques famous artists use." I pause, waiting for the shower of anger to pound down on me, but Chee is silent.

He does not notice the drawings tacked on the bulletin board, but he does notice the book on my nightstand. "What's that?"

"A diary," I say. "Mom bought it for me for my birthday so I can write down the stories I tell my sisters."

He nods, taking in the words, but not saying anything in return.

I wonder if he is building up his anger, waiting to explode like a volcano. I shudder and rub my arms, as if I am cold.

"What's in that box?"

"My dolls," I say, shoving the box back into the closet. "I took them down to make room for the books."

He nods. "Looks like you're growing up."

I study him with suspicion. He hobbles into the room and perches on the edge of the mattress next to the essay I wanted to show him. For a moment, I think about mentioning it to him, but he smells of cleaning supplies and sick people, and I feel my chest constrict with sorrow.

He folds his hands between his knees and purses his lips.

Uh-oh, I think, *here comes the lecture.*

He takes a few shallow breaths.

Be a tree, I remind myself. *Whatever he says, bend, don't break.*

His voice starts like a gentle breeze. "You know I expect a lot from you and your sisters," he says, "but I want you to know I only expect the best so I can get the best out of you. Not to punish you and make you miserable."

I wonder why he is telling me this, but I don't say anything. I sit back on my heels and imagine my body the sturdy trunk of a tree, rooted deep in the soil. I listen. Chee's words rustle against me.

"When I was in the hospital, I started to worry about what would happen if I died. I know it's not nice to think about, but someday I won't be around to take care of you. Then you'll have to get a job. Do you want to flip burgers at McDonald's or do you want to work in an office with air-conditioning?"

Without thinking, I say the truth, "I want to draw."

"What a waste of time." His words batter against me like a brisk, hollow wind. "I'm not talking about what you want to do. I'm talking about what you need to do to pay the bills, to survive."

I whisper, "Aren't there jobs that require drawing?"

"They don't pay much."

"Money isn't everything."

"It makes life easier," he says. "Don't you want your life to be easy?"

When I don't answer, he takes my silence as defiance.

He glances at my face, then at the carpet. His brown eyes flicker with inspiration. He slaps his thighs and smiles. "You get good grades, right? Well, maybe you go to best college in the world on scholarship. Maybe you meet a rich man and marry him."

"I might meet another guy on scholarship," I say. "Then he would be just as poor as I am."

"Aiyaah! You not listening."

I stand up. "Maybe I don't want to get married," I spit. "Maybe I want to be single and travel around the world in a hot air balloon."

He lifts his eyebrows in surprise. "You do?"

I shake my head. His words have stirred my memory. I think of what Lammie Pie said about Chee's ulcer, how he is still trapped by his mother's demands, although he is old enough to live as he chooses. I don't want to live like him. I want my life to be different. I don't want to be the Scarecrow from *The Wizard of Oz* like Cynthia said I am. I want to think for myself. And I can't wait to start learning how to do it when I'm eighteen like the beautician said to do. I need to start now.

I take a deep breath. My hands tremble, but my body is firm. "You don't understand," I say. "What you want for me is not what I want for myself. And if you die and I continue to live my life for you, then I might as well be dead, too, because I won't be who I am meant to be. I won't be real. I won't be happy."

"You aren't happy?"

I swallow hard. What would happen if I told the truth?

He continues to patiently stare at me, waiting for my answer.

I think of Cinderella on the bulletin board, the art books on the shelf, the hours I have spent scribbling in my diary. I think of packing lunches, helping my sisters with their homework, tucking them in at night. I think of my mother in the kitchen eating Danish cookies and worrying about getting fat. I think of my father lying in a hospital bed wondering whether or not he is going to die. I think of happiness, what it is, what it means.

"Sometimes," I say.

Deep lines crease his forehead. "What makes you happy?"

I inhale deeply, feeling a surge of strength. "Drawing," I tell him. "And writing."

He shakes his head with disappointment.

My spine tenses. *Whatever he says, do not break.*

For a minute, he sits with his head bent, lips pursed, staring at the carpet. Finally, he sighs and lifts his head although he does not look at me. "I worry about you and your sisters. I don't want any one of you to have to struggle to pay bills or put food on the table or buy nice things." He stares at his feet. "I know I'm not perfect. I've made mistakes. I lie, I cheat, I steal. I flirt too much. I boss Lammie Pie around. I scold you and your sisters. But I don't mean to hurt anyone. That's not my intention. I just want your life to be better than mine. More stable. More secure. More successful. That's why I want you and your sisters to do well in school, to marry rich, to live a fabulous life without having to worry about anything." He glances up at me, and there are tears in his eyes. "But I also want you to be happy." He sits up and notices the drawings on the bulletin board. His face hardens. I hold my breath. He shifts on the mattress, struggling to get up, and his hand plunges into the essay, crumpling the paper. His gaze shifts to the wrinkled essay and his face softens when he notices the grade I received. He glances up at the drawings on the bulletin board, then down at the crumpled essay.

Chee purses his lips and says, "Mah-Mah didn't approve of Lammie Pie when she met her. She wanted me to marry a Chinese woman. But I married Lammie Pie anyway because I knew she was the one for me. Now, Mah-Mah says Lammie Pie is the best daughter-in-law she has. And she is the only one who is not Chinese."

I am dumbfounded.

His jaw twitches with tension. "Maybe I worry over nothing. You're smart and talented. Maybe you can find a way to be happy and successful."

My heart flutters in my chest. "Are you saying I have your permission to draw?"

"No, this is not about permission." His unwavering gaze penetrates me. "I'm saying sometimes we have to do things no one else understands. And I want you to know that even when I disagree with you, I still love you."

My eyes mist. "How can you love me if you don't approve of my drawing?"

"Someday, if you have kids, you'll understand," he says.

"But I don't want to wait that long." *I want to know everything. Right now.*

He pats his lap, indicating he wants me to sit down like a child. I cross my arms over my chest and remain standing. He looks sad and defeated, but I don't care anymore.

"I can't give you my blessing for something I disapprove of," he says. "I think drawing is a waste of time. But obviously, you don't, or you would have stopped a long time ago without me having to ask you to."

"So, are you saying you want me to drop my painting class next semester?"

"I'm saying I want you to be happy and successful. If drawing makes you happy, draw. If writing makes you happy, write. If you're lucky and you have what it takes, you'll succeed just like you do in school."

I guess that's close enough, I think.

He opens up his arms and tries to smile. He wants me to be happy. He wants me to be successful. Maybe someday when I am a rich and famous artist he'll be proud of me. Just like Mah-Mah is proud to have Lammie Pie as her daughter-in-law.

I wrap my arms around his back and kiss his cheek.

He rubs my back and whispers, "Remember, I always love you."

The tightness in my chest loosens. "I love you, too. And I'm glad you're healthy. It's good to have you home."

17: A CHINESE CHRISTMAS

A month later, Lammie Pie convinces Chee to host the annual Christmas party at our house. "No traveling for us," she reasons. "No stress. No Mah-Mah."

"I have to invite my mother," Chee says. "You don't understand. She'll write us out of the will."

"We've never been in the will, remember? We have only daughters, not sons."

"I can't leave her all alone," Chee reasons, "not on Christmas."

"She won't be alone. Uncle John and Aunt Lil already volunteered to spend it with her. They're taking her to St. Mary's Cathedral for midnight Mass and then out to breakfast."

Chee sighs. It's settled. The Lams will travel to our house on Christmas Eve.

The day after Thanksgiving, Chee loads us into the van to shop for the perfect Christmas tree. We travel to Doug's Christmas Tree Orchard. I pick out a Douglas fir. "Too tall," Chee says. Cynthia selects a pine. "Too short," Chee says. Elizabeth finds one she likes. It's a scrawny, lopsided fir with half its needles gone. Cynthia snickers, "Are you crazy? Dad won't go for that." Elizabeth pouts. "But it's just like Charlie Brown's tree." When Chee walks through the maze and finds us standing by the droopy tree, he yells, "Aiyaah! Don't you know anything? That's not a tree; that's a shrub. What will everyone say?"

"But I like this one," Elizabeth sobs.

"You can't have everything you like. I like money, but you don't see me taking it out of everyone's wallet. C'mon. We'll go to another place to find a tree."

But the second tree farm has even less to choose from.

"Aiyaah!" Chee revs the engine and almost backs into a man carrying a fir over his shoulder. Its green bristles rub against the windows of the van. Chee rolls down his window and shouts profanity in Cantonese. "Next time watch where you're going!"

The man with the tree keeps walking.

Chee shakes his head. "People have no manners."

"Pedestrians always have the right of way," Lammie Pie explains. "You should slow down and keep your eyes on the road."

Chee drives in silence. He has learned to not argue with Lammie Pie. A few minutes later, we spot a third tree farm. Chee pulls into the dirt parking lot. Plumes of dust cloud the windows. Chee grumbles, "I'm going to have to wash the van again."

Hand in hand, we walk through the maze of trees, examining each one carefully for color, texture, and fullness. "How long this one last?" Chee asks a clerk.

The man rolls up his checkered shirt sleeves and bends down to lift the trunk. "See here." He points to the rings on the bottom of the trunk. "Keep this moist and it'll last four to six weeks."

"You have to water it?" Chee asks.

Lammie Pie nudges him in the ribs. "You stick the trunk in a bowl of water like you stick flowers in a vase."

Chee nods, pretending he knows. He points to a six-foot fir tree covered with deep-green bristles. "How much?"

"Fifteen dollars."

"For a tree?"

"You go try cutting one down yourself, Chinaman. I'll bet you $10 you'll come running back to buy that tree from me."

"Just pay the man," Lammie Pie hisses. She doesn't wait for Chee to withdraw his wallet. She rifles through the pockets of her leather purse and removes a twenty-dollar bill from her checkbook.

"Thank you, ma'am," the man says, winking. His gaze lingers

a moment too long on her face, and Lammie Pie smiles and turns away, blushing.

Chee asks the man if he will help him strap the tree to the top of the van.

"That's an extra ten dollars."

"Ten dollars?"

Lammie Pie says, "Never mind, we'll do it." She bends down to grab the tree by the trunk, but the man in the checkered shirt stops her by putting his fingers on the back of her hand.

"Let me take care of that," he says, smiling at her.

"She's my wife, you know," Chee says.

"The woman has a mouth. Let her speak," the man says. He winks at Lammie Pie and hoists the tree on his back and carries it to the van. With a ladder, he climbs up on the hood and straps the branches to the sides of the vehicle. "Should hold pretty good. Just make sure you use a knife to cut the rope loose and that you park on a level spot so the tree won't slide back and hit you."

"Thanks again." Lammie Pie flashes a smile. Her blue eyes sparkle like sapphires.

The man helps us back the van out of the dirt parking lot. He waves good-bye. Lammie Pie blows a kiss.

"Don't encourage him," Chee says. "You're married. What type of example are you showing the girls?"

Lammie Pie's eyes narrow. "It's no different than the one you're always showing them."

"Not true. I never blow a kiss."

"No, but you've kissed the store girls' hands."

"That's to trick them into giving me a good deal. Nothing else."

"Well, I think we got a good deal. We saved $10."

Chee grunts, but does not say a word.

Cynthia titters. Elizabeth and I smile.

———

At home, Chee climbs into the rafters of the garage and removes three large cardboard boxes full of ornaments Lammie Pie made before she became a mother. Cynthia, Elizabeth, and I kneel by the tree and watch Lammie Pie remove the lids and lift crocheted snowflakes, ceramic angels, wooden sleds, felt stockings, cotton-ball teddy bears, and Styrofoam snowmen from the dusty box. Lammie Pie hands us the sturdier pieces for us to place on the lower branches.

After the tree is decorated, Chee turns up the music. Frank Sinatra sings "Here Comes Santa Claus." Chee grabs Lammie Pie around the waist and twirls her around the living room. The hard lines of her face blossom into a smile. My sisters and I step back and give them room. Their feet glide across the carpet and their bodies sway in time with the music and each other. When they finish dancing, Chee kisses Lammie Pie, and she lets his lips linger against her mouth instead of pushing him away.

———

The week before Christmas, everyone except Lammie Pie gets sick. Chee, Cynthia, Elizabeth, and I have runny noses, watery eyes, and itchy throats that will not go away no matter what over-the-counter medications we use. On Christmas Eve morning, Chee packs Cynthia, Elizabeth, and me into the van and drives a half hour to the emergency room at Kaiser. The double doors slide open. A sterile smell wafts over us. We patter across the spotless linoleum floors to the reception area. The nurse lifts her glasses and eyes us. "Burns or broken bones?" she asks. Chee shakes his head. "Gunshot wounds or deep knife cuts?" Chee shakes his head again. The nurse hands him back our medical identification cards. "Sounds like it's not an emergency, sir. I'm sorry, but you'll have to make an appointment during regular business hours."

Chee grips the ledge of the counter and tries to sweet talk the nurse into letting us be seen. "It is an emergency," he explains. "It's Christmas Eve and my daughter's supposed to sing and just listen to her voice." Elizabeth opens her mouth and belts out a hoarse, "Have Yourself a Merry Little Christmas." The nurse shakes her head. "Sorry, I can't help. Next please."

Chee bends his head down and shuffles down the wide corridor. Outside, sirens blast. Moments later, the double doors slide open and a gurney is wheeled down the hall by two paramedics. Cynthia, Elizabeth, and I press our backs against the wall, letting them pass.

The swinging doors beside the reception area push forward and a man in a white hospital coat whistles. Chee rushes toward him. "Doc?"

The man glances up, his lips still puckered.

"My daughters are sick. Can you look at them?"

He motions toward the receptionist. "I'm sure they can help you at the front desk. The sooner you register, the less of a wait you'll have. Now, if you'll excuse me, I'm on my way to lunch."

Chee grabs his arm. "Please, doc, it'll only take a minute. My daughters are supposed to sing and just listen to their voices."

Cynthia, Elizabeth, and I open our mouths and sing, "Have Yourself a Merry Little Christmas."

The doctor scratches his chin, and then tells us to open our mouths again. He peeks inside and nods. "Allergies," he says. "Do you own a Christmas tree?"

"Yes," Chee says, puffing up his chest. "Best on the block."

"Get rid of it," the doctor says. "It's making all of you sick."

Heartbroken, Chee obeys the doctor. He opens the sliding glass door and carries the tree into the backyard. With an orange extension cord, he plugs the lights into a socket. Red, yellow, blue, and white lights twinkle. Elizabeth presses her nose against the window, fogging up the glass. Chee smacks her shoulder. "Just look. Don't touch." Elizabeth obeys. When Chee leaves the room to wash his hands, Elizabeth opens her mouth and breathes on the glass until a frosted circle as big as her face appears. Cynthia laughs.

Although I hate having the tree outside, the doctor is right. Our noses stop running. Our eyes clear up. We can sing. Cynthia will be able to tap dance without sniffing back tears. Elizabeth will be able to belt out, "Have Yourself a Merry Little Christmas," without sounding like a toad. And, I won't have to look like Rudolph with my nose rubbed raw from tissue.

Only Lammie Pie objects to the tree being outside. "What if it rains?"

"It's under the patio awning," Chee explains. "It's safe."

But Lammie Pie knows better. "What if the wind blows?"

Chee says nothing. He has no reasons to give her, at least, none she will believe. He decides to keep his mouth shut.

———

At a quarter to five, the Lams arrive for dinner. My sisters and I greet everyone with hugs and kisses. We take their coats and purses and place them on the quilted comforter of our parents' queen-size bed. Red envelopes stuffed with dollar bills are thrust into our hands. We linger in the living room, waiting for Chee's cue for us to entertain. But no one cares about us. Uncles and aunts and cousins hover over the buffet table nibbling at Lammie Pie's award-winning baked goods and homemade Chinese food. No one asks us about school. No one wants to see Cynthia dance. No one wants to hear us sing. They walk past us through the living room, searching for the Christmas tree.

"You don't have a tree?" Uncle Bill asks, licking his sticky fingers from one of the bow ties.

"I think I saw lights outside," Aunt Lucy says, pointing to the sliding glass door in the family room.

Uncle Bill steps down into the family room and lifts his glasses. He bends forward and touches his forehead against the window. "That your tree?"

Chee nods.

"Why outside?" Uncle Bill asks.

"It was making the girls sick. The doctor said to get rid of it, but I couldn't throw it away. I paid good money for it. So I put it outside."

"What did Dave do this time?" Uncle Jimmy asks, ambling into the family room.

"He put the Christmas tree outside." Uncle Bill points to the winking lights behind the glass.

"Really, Dave? Why'd you do that? You want us to go outside to open gifts? Too cheap to get your carpets cleaned if we spill something?" Uncle Jimmy laughs. "Hey, Mary, come look at this."

Aunt Mary walks out of the kitchen, drying her hands on a dishcloth. "What's the fuss?"

"Uncle Dave put the Christmas tree outside."

"Why'd you do that?"

"We got sick. Runny noses, watery eyes. Doctor said we're allergic to tree. So, instead of getting rid of it, I put it outside."

"Clever, Dave," Aunt Mary says. "You've always been clever." Chee smiles.

After dinner, we sit in the living room and open our gifts. Most of the packages contain the same items we get every year: school supplies or winter jackets or board games we can play together. In the middle of unwrapping gifts, the phone rings. Lammie Pie strolls into the living room. "It's Uncle John," she says. "Who wants to speak with him first?"

I raise my hand and take the phone from her. "Hi, Uncle John," I say. "Thanks for the purple robe." He usually sends each of us a hundred-dollar bill in a fancy card, but this year he sent actual gifts, which he bought. When Chee saw the robes, he muttered, "So ugly, so cheap, probably made in China." Then, when he thought no one was listening, he whispered to Lammie Pie, "What did we do to make him not like us anymore?"

I don't tell Uncle John what I overheard my father say. Instead, I share only my enthusiasm when he asks if the robe fits. "It's perfect."

"I'm sorry Aunt Lil and I aren't there tonight," he says. "I would have liked to have seen you and your sisters in the robes."

"Maybe I can get someone to take a picture and send it to you."

"Ah, yes, that would be good." He pauses. "I want you to know I didn't give money this year because I've sponsored a hungry child in Africa."

I twirl the phone cord around my wrist and smile. "That's okay," I say, thinking of the tiny pink flowers embroidered around the cuffs. "I'm not my father. I don't live for money."

He laughs. "You're right. You don't." He waits another second before he says, "Aunt Lil and I could not have children because of her health, but if we did have children, we would have wanted a daughter like you."

"Not a son?"

"No," Uncle John says. "No son would be as good as you."

I smile. Soft warmth radiates from my chest and flows into my arms. "That's the kindest thing you've ever said."

"I mean it," he reassures me. "You're a remarkable young lady."

I give the phone to my sisters. When they are done, they give the phone to Chee. He takes the receiver and speaks to Uncle John in English, then in Cantonese. I do not understand what he is saying, but his voice is getting louder. Then he stops talking. His face changes again. There is a softness in his cheeks, a slackness to his jaw. He covers his eyes with his other hand and says in Cantonese, "I love you, too, Mah-Mah." That much I understand.

18: Art Class

When school starts in January, I am officially enrolled in Mr. Rochette's 2D art class. I share a table with Todd and Tim, two African-American boys who are twins. They share everything, from their colored pencils to their sketchbook. I feel like an outsider sitting at their table, but they say they don't mind me. "We aren't shy like you," Todd says, flashing a smile.

I blush.

Mr. Rochette is tall and angular with long dirty-blond hair that falls straight to his shoulders except for a bald patch on the back of his head. He wears bright Hawaiian shirts and khaki slacks with leather sandals. His artwork is displayed in the class. "I've been all around the world painting," he says, bringing out his slide show and turning off the lights.

I stare at the tourist attractions in Europe and wonder how it would feel to walk along the cobblestone streets and glance up into the same sky van Gogh painted years and years ago.

"Any questions?" Mr. Rochette asks, turning on the lights.

I raise my hand. "Did you see van Gogh's self-portraits in the Louvre?"

Mr. Rochette wrinkles his nose. "I prefer cubism over impressionism."

"What's he talking about?" I ask the twins.

Todd leans across the desk and whispers, "Picasso."

"Was he European?" I ask.

"No, he was modern," Tim says.

I sigh. *So much to learn.*

The first week of class, we study perspective. I draw a railroad track from one point perspective, a city from two-point perspective, and a farmhouse from three-point perspective.

Mr. Rochette sniffs across my shoulder. "Something's not right." He wrinkles his nose. "Try giving it texture."

"Texture?" But he is already across the room critiquing another student's work.

I ask Todd and Tim to interpret, but they are so absorbed in their joint sketch of an amusement park that they have failed to hear the conversation.

By the middle of the semester, we start painting. Todd and Tim have a professional watercolor set they purchased with their allowance money. The rest of the class uses the bright, crusty poster paints supplied by the school. We've all chosen a picture that we've previously drawn to fill with color. I have sketched a fish in the sea. Todd and Tim have chosen a picture of their dog. I watch with envy as Todd and Tim mix the moist, luscious colors from the small tubes of paint on a wooden palate and smear it over their canvas. I stare down at my hard, bright color palate and try to mix the colors so they are soft but not too watery. At first, the colors dribble from my brush. Then, the paints stick too much. Finally, on the third try, I get the color and the consistency right.

Mr. Rochette glances over my shoulder and sniffs. "You must like failure," he says.

"What?" I ask, my brush in midair.

He lifts his eyebrows and nods at my sketch. "As a beginning student, I would have never selected a fish in water for my first painting. Don't you know flesh and water are the two most difficult things to paint? Even professionals struggle with it."

I am silent. When he leaves, I dip my brush into the yellow mixture and begin to paint.

At the end of class, Mr. Rochette circles around the room to examine our work. He stops at my table and sniffs. "You paint pretty well, don't you?"

I don't know if he means it as a compliment or a question. The bell rings before I can ask.

Toward the end of the semester, Mr. Rochette announces a painting contest. It's open to all students enrolled in any art class from all the schools in the district.

Todd and Tim nudge me. "You should enter your fish," they say.

I glance at the wall where Mr. Rochette displays the best work of his students. My fish is wedged between a painting of a school and Todd and Tim's portrait of their dog.

"You might win," Todd says.

I shrug. "You both are better artists."

"You're better than you think," Tim says.

At the end of class, Mr. Rochette approaches me with a slip of paper and a pen. "I need your permission to enter your watercolor in the contest."

I shake my head. "I want to take it home."

"You can take it home after the contest," he says. "The contest ends a week before school is out. You can come by the office and pick it up, okay?"

I think about it for a while before I agree to sign the document.

A week before school ends, Chee notices my name in the paper while I am eating breakfast. "You won fifty dollars for a watercolor," he says, folding the paper in half. "Why you not tell me?"

My eyes widen. *I won?* "I didn't know I'd won anything."

"Look. It says your name right here." Chee stands up and walks down the hall to his bedroom and returns with his coupon-cutting scissors so he can save the article. "What you paint?"

My eyes scan the paper, searching for my name. Chee's right. It's there.

I hand the paper back to him. "A fish."

"A fish?"

"It was a class assignment," I explain. "I got in trouble for choosing an underwater scene. Mr. Rochette said it was too hard."

"Too hard? Not too hard for you. You won first place." Chee

smiles. "Wait till I tell Lammie Pie and your sisters. They'll be just as proud as I am." He stands up and kisses my cheek. Waving the paper above his head, he shuffles into the living room. "Fifty dollars," I hear him say.

I shake my head. *All he cares about is money.*

The next day, I go to the office to collect my painting and the fifty dollars, but the secretary says Mr. Rochette already picked them up. When I get to the classroom, the door is locked. I squint through the tiny window in the door and see Mr. Rochette floating around the room from table to table just as he does when he teaches class. But the classroom is empty. I pound on the door until he answers.

"Yes?" he asks, gazing down at me.

"I'm here for my fish," I say.

He shakes his head. "I told you to try the office."

"I did and the secretary sent me here."

"I'm sorry," he says. "But I don't have it."

After school, I tell Chee what happened. He calls the school and speaks with the principal who speaks with Mr. Rochette. An hour later, the principal calls to tell Chee nobody knows what happened to the painting or the money.

"You steal fifty dollars from my innocent daughter," Chee says on the phone.

I slink out of the room and sit cross-legged on my bed and hold my Chow dog radio to my chest. I think of all the things Chee has stolen over the years, things that belonged to someone else, things he pretended he needed more than the rightful owners did. And now people are stealing from me. *It's not fair,* I think, feeling my stomach growl with anger.

I glance out my window at the orange tree in the backyard that Chee planted for good luck. I think of our house, painted red and gold for happiness and good luck. I sadly realize luck, whether good or bad, is something beyond my control.

What if the principal is right, and no one knows what happened to my fish, I think. *What if it got sent to the wrong school and someone picked it up instead of returning it. Then it will be gone forever.*

I stare at my bulletin board, at the space I made for the fish. The hole gapes like a lost front tooth.

I want my fish back, I think. *He would have a good home in my bedroom. My walls are blue, as blue as the sea.*

In the kitchen, I hear Chee hang up the phone. His footsteps pad across the linoleum and down the hall to my bedroom. I clutch my Chow dog radio and stare at the gap on my bulletin board. *So what if the fish is gone?* I think. *I will paint other pictures.*

ACKNOWLEDGMENTS

I would like to thank Brooke Warner of She Writes Press and Regina Brooks of Serendipity Literary Agency for sponsoring the 2014 Memoir Discovery Contest. I am grateful for being chosen as the inaugural winner.

I would like to thank everyone at She Writes Press for working with me to make this book a success.

Thanks to my amazing publicist, Eva Zimmerman, for always being a phone call away.

Special thanks to the people and institutions who shepherded this book from its conception: Maureen Sullivan, who believed in this book enough to edit it and who taught me the power of writing through tears; the staff at *The Sun,* who published an excerpt from the book titled, "Red Eggs"; the staff at Copperfield's Books in Santa Rosa, who published an excerpt from the book, "The Makeover," in their annual *Dickens* literary magazine; and to the San Francisco Intersection for the Arts and the San Francisco Foundation for awarding the first draft of the manuscript the 2003 Mary Tanenbaum Award for Creative Nonfiction.

Thanks to the writers who continue to inspire me, especially Geoff Wood, Melanie Rae Thon, and Jennifer Lynn Alvarez.

Thanks to my family. Where the book ends, the story continues. My father has surprised me with his own red-egg transformation. I appreciate his unconditional love and faith. He is an inspiration to his grandchildren. My mother, who supported my writing by paying for my initial subscription to *Writer's Digest*, continues to encourage me. My sisters have been one of the greatest joys and blessings of my life, including the youngest, who was born after the events chronicled in this book. Thanks also to my uncles, aunts, and cousins, who enrich my life.

Thanks to my daughter, who continually reminds me to be a star. And a special thank you to my son, who has no words. He has turned my life inside out and shown me the importance of being humble, compassionate, grounded, and peaceful by focusing on what matters most.

Lastly, my eternal gratitude to Ed Turpin for supporting my writing career for over 25 years. Ed has accepted awards on my behalf and spoken at readings for me. He has also endured being called, "The Poet's Husband," after a short story by Molly Giles. Without his encouragement, *Red Eggs and Good Luck* would have remained a file on my computer. No matter what the future holds, I will always cherish Ed's sacrifices and contributions. I will keep his belief in me and my talents close to my heart.

ABOUT THE AUTHOR

© Rose Turpin

Angela Lam is a writer and an artist, who lives in Northern California. She is the author of a collection of short stories, *The Human Act and Other Stories*, and three novels published under Angela Lam Turpin. *Red Eggs and Good Luck* won the 2003 Mary Tanenbaum Award for creative nonfiction and the 2014 Memoir Discovery Contest.

SELECTED TITLES FROM SHE WRITES PRESS

She Writes Press is an independent publishing company
founded to serve women writers everywhere.
Visit us at www.shewritespress.com.

Her Name Is Kaur: Sikh American Women Write About Love, Courage, and Faith edited by Meeta Kaur $17.95, 978-1-938314-70-4
An eye-opening, multifaceted collection of essays by Sikh American women exploring the concept of love in the context of the modern landscape and influences that shape their lives.

The S-Word by Paolina Milana
$16.95, 978-1-63152-927-6
An insider's account of growing up with a schizophrenic mother, and the disastrous toll the illness—and her Sicilian Catholic family's code of secrecy—takes upon her young life.

The Coconut Latitudes: Secrets, Storms, and Survival in the Caribbean by Rita Gardner $16.95, 978-1-63152-901-6
A haunting, lyrical memoir about a dysfunctional family's experiences in a reality far from the envisioned Eden—and the terrible cost of keeping secrets.

A Different Kind of Same: A Memoir by Kelley Clink
$16.95, 978-1-63152-999-3
Several years before Kelley Clink's brother hanged himself, she attempted suicide by overdose. In the aftermath of his death, she traces the evolution of both their illnesses, and wonders: If he couldn't make it, what hope is there for her?

Don't Call Me Mother: A Daughter's Journey from Abandonment to Forgiveness by Linda Joy Myers $16.95, 978-1-938314-02-5
Linda Joy Myers's story of how she transcended the prisons of her childhood by seeking—and offering—forgiveness for her family's sins.

The Outskirts of Hope: A Memoir by Jo Ivester
$16.95, 978-1-63152-964-1
A moving, inspirational memoir about how living and working in an all-black town during the height of the civil rights movement profoundly affected the author's entire family—and how they in turn impacted the community.